# ELM CREEK QUILTS

## QUILT PROJECTS INSPIRED *by the* ELM CREEK QUILTS NOVELS

Jennifer Chiaverini & Nancy Odom

C&T PUBLISHING

© 2002 by Jennifer Chiaverini and Nancy Odom

Editor: Cyndy Lyle Rymer

Technical Editors: Carolyn Aune and Gael Betts

Copyeditor/Proofreader: Susan Nelson

Cover Designer: Kristen Yenche

Design Director/Book Designer: Kristen Yenche

Illustrator: Nancy Odom and Jeffery Carillo

Production Assistant: Tim Manibusan

Photography: Sharon Risedorph unless otherwise noted

Published by C&T Publishing, Inc., P.O. Box 1456, Lafayette, California 94549

Front cover: *Elm Creek Medallion* by Jennifer Chiaverini

Back cover: *Sarah's Sampler* and *The Runaway Quilt* by Jennifer Chiaverini

Library of Congress Cataloging-in-Publication Data

Chiaverini, Jennifer.

Elm Creek quilts : projects inspired by the Elm Creek quilts novels /

Jennifer Chiaverini and Nancy Odom.

p.

Includes index.

ISBN 1-57120-177-7 (paper trade)

1. Patchwork—Patterns. 2. Quilting. 3. Patchwork quilts. 4.

Chiaverini, Jennifer—Introduction. I. Odom, Nancy II. Title.

TT835 .C453 2002

746.46'041—dc21

2002007380

Printed in China

ISBN 1-57120-177-7

10 9 8 7 6 5 4 3 2 1

# DEDICATION

To the Mad City Quilters, the quilters of RCTQ, and all loyal fans of the Elm Creek Quilts novels.

—*Jennifer Chiaverini*

Thank you...
to my husband, Jim, for his constant encouragement, friendship, and support..
He's a true eternal companion (and a pretty fun business partner, too!).

to my children (and now grandchildren) for sharing their lives and space with fabric, scissors, rotary cutters, rulers, batting, sewing machines, and all the other things that go along with this addiction. They always have been and continue to be an integral part of all my life's adventures.

to all my friends in the quilting industry. You inspire me and motivate me day and night with your support and creativity. It's such fun and truly an honor to be included in such a wonderful circle.

to all the quilters around the world who enjoy my designs. Thank you for the constant kind words, uplifting stories, and the occasional photographs. It's thrilling to know that the joy I find in what I do has found its way into your hearts as well.

—*Nancy Odom*

# TABLE of

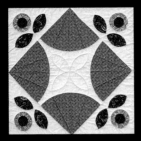

# CONTENTS

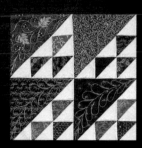

## From *The Runaway Quilt*

# FOREWORD

As fans of Jennifer's Elm Creek Quilts novels, we have spent many hours vicariously enjoying the comings and goings of the many wonderful characters. It's fun to look back on the circumstances that led to the birth of this book, since the idea for the book came from a brainstorming session while at a quilt camp. Joyce Lytle, C&T's senior technical editor, suggested one morning that C&T needed to do a book based on Jennifer's novels. We jumped all over the idea. We decided to contact Jennifer, and as soon as we returned from quilt camp we contacted Jennifer to see if she would be interested. Jennifer called the next morning, and we were off and quilting.

A few more brainstorming sessions later, and a list of potential quilts inspired by the four novels Jennifer has shared with her readers had grown to enough for a couple of books. Amazingly enough, despite Jennifer's busy (!) life as a mother, writer, quilter, etc., she was able to make seven of the quilts featured. These include *Sarah's Sampler* from *The Quilter's Apprentice*, the *Elm Creek Medallion* that graces the cover of this book from *Round Robin*, *Cross-Country Challenge* from *The Cross-Country Quilters*, and *Birds in the Air*, *The Runaway Quilt*, and *The Underground Railroad Quilt* from *The Runaway Quilt*. *Gerda's Log Cabin Quilt* is a special case: Jennifer invited her fans to make Log Cabin blocks, and received a tremendous response. Contributors are listed on page 79.

Nancy Odom, owner of Timid Thimble Creations, designer of the Quilter's Gloves, and creative genius, was called in to help us design and make *Sylvia's Broken Star*, *Andrew's Star in the Window*, *When He Makes Dinner*, *Vinnie's Double Pinwheel*, and *Joanna's Pumpkins and Pomegranates*.

It has been a pleasure working with Jennifer and Nancy to create a book we all hope you enjoy. In the meantime, maybe we'll see you at quilt camp! Quilting friends truly *are* the best friends anyone could ask for.

Cyndy Lyle Rymer and Joyce Lytle
Editors

# INTRODUCTION

Ever since I learned to read, I have longed to create stories and share them with readers as my favorite authors had shared their stories with me. For nearly that long, I have also admired and appreciated quilts, but I never imagined that my love for quilting would one day allow me to fulfill my lifelong dream of becoming a novelist.

In June of 1994, I married Martin Chiaverini, whom I had met three years before in an undergraduate creative writing course at the University of Notre Dame. We lived in State College, Pennsylvania, where he worked toward his Ph.D. in mechanical engineering at Penn State and I taught part-time for the English department—and struggled to launch my writing career. Although my new teaching position allowed me time to write, I could not get beyond the first page of any story I attempted-ed. The resulting frustration made it difficult to persevere, and every time I sat down at the computer and tried to start something new, I had to ignore the voices of doubt and fear that whispered this was one dream I would not fulfill.

*Jennifer and Martin Chiaverini on their wedding day. St. James of the Valley Church. Cincinnati, OH, June 25, 1994.*
Photo credit: Craycroft Studios

Fortunately, I was able to forget my writer's block in the excitement surrounding our wedding. In the midst of the plans and preparations, I found myself longing for a beautiful heirloom wedding quilt to commemorate the occasion and brighten up the apartment we would soon share. Unfortunately, I had no friends or relatives who quilted and could be counted on to make us a quilt for a wedding gift, nor did our tight budget allow us to purchase one. Before long it became obvious that if I wanted a beautiful heirloom wedding quilt, I would have to make it myself.

At that time, State College did not have a quilt shop, so I bought an instruction book and fabric from a discount store and taught myself to quilt. My first project was a simple nine-block sampler wall-hanging, not the elaborate king-size bed quilt I had envisioned, but I was so pleased with it that I wanted to begin a new project immediately. I purchased more books, browsed through quilting magazines at the library, and met other quilters on the Internet.

My passion for quilting grew, and as soon as I saved up enough money for a sewing machine, I taught myself machine piecing and rotary-cutting techniques. My second quilt was a Lone Star wallhanging for Marty's parents, and after that, I made a Jacob's Ladder quilt for my mother's Christmas present. In the years that followed, I made many more quilts, some large, some small, some for decoration, and some to cuddle my cousins' newborns.

I still have not made that beautiful heirloom wedding quilt, but I can picture it clearly. To celebrate my tenth quilting anniversary—as well as our tenth wedding anniversary, since they fall within a month

*Jennifer and Nicholas Chiaverini in Mukwonago, WI on the* Round Robin *book tour. Photo credit: Martin Chiaverini.*

of each other—I plan to make a "Dear Jennifer" quilt, taking my inspiration from the well-known "Dear Jane" quilts. I would like to make a sampler of six-inch blocks including all of the blocks I have made in my first ten years as a quilter. This is quite an ambitious project, so I have already warned Marty that our "Dear Jennifer" quilt might not be on the bed until our twentieth anniversary!

The summer of 1994 passed. Autumn found me enjoying my life as a newlywed, teaching at Penn State, quilting—and still stumbling through the first pages of my novel. I knew what I wanted to write; I knew the mood, the theme, and I even had a vague idea about two of the characters, a young woman and her older and wiser friend. Yet I struggled to get beyond the first few paragraphs of any story I started.

I wanted to write about women and their work, and about valuing the work we as women choose to do. Too many women I knew disparaged their work. Many working mothers thought they ought to be home with their children instead, and so they carried around too much guilt to enjoy their jobs. Mothers who chose to stay home to care for their children thought they ought to be working outside the home, too. Many of my single friends, pursuing exciting careers they had studied and worked for years to obtain, thought they should be doing some-

thing more lucrative, something more important, or just something else. This saddened me. I believe that if our work is worth the time, energy, and talent we commit to it, we ought to value it, especially if we expect other people to do the same. If we don't value this work to which we turn over so much of our lives, then we ought to do something else.

Friendship was another theme I wanted to explore, especially women's friendships and the way women use friendship to sustain themselves and nurture each other. I wanted to include this theme in my first novel not only as a tribute to the most important friendships of my own life, but also out of a sense of longing for the friendships that I could not find when I needed them most.

Though I knew what I wanted to write about, I could not bring those two disparate themes together. I tried writing about jobs I had had and enjoyed (teaching, or my first real job as a page at the Thousand Oaks (CA) City Library) as well as jobs that had not been quite so satisfying. Regardless of what I attempted, I could not wrestle those two themes into a coherent story.

Then, at last, I realized the answer had been right in front of me all along: I should write about quilters. Anyone who works on a quilt, who devotes her time, energy, creativity, and passion to that art, learns to

*Jennifer and Nicholas on a book tour stop in Cincinnati, OH. Photo credit: Martin Chiaverini.*

value the work of her hands. And as any quilter will tell you, a quilter's quilting friends are some of the dearest, most generous, and most supportive people she knows. Two quilters who have just met will be strangers only until their mutual passion for quilting is revealed. Then they can talk for hours like the best of friends. Quilting wove together my two themes like no other subject could, and since beginning writers are often told to "write what you know," I realized I had finally found my story.

*Nicholas Chiaverini on the Pineapple quilt Jennifer made for him. June 2000. Photo credit: Jennifer Chiaverini.*

After working on *The Quilter's Apprentice* for so long in solitude, and struggling to get it into print, I was gratified to discover how much readers from around the world enjoyed the story of Sylvia and Sarah. I had hoped readers would be touched by the characters I had created, but I never could have imagined that they would come to look on Sarah, Sylvia, and the Elm Creek Quilters as friends.

I never intended to write a series or even a sequel to *The Quilter's Apprentice*. Like most authors, I assumed I would move on to new settings, characters, and themes in my subsequent novels. But the reaction to *The Quilter's Apprentice* was so positive that I decided to continue the story of Elm Creek Manor in a second volume, *Round Robin*.

In *Round Robin*, I explored two questions that remained unanswered from *The Quilter's Apprentice*. First, I wanted to see if Sarah and Sylvia were, in fact, able to fulfill their grand plan to turn Elm Creek Manor, Sylvia's ancestral home, into a retreat for quilters. All Sarah and Sylvia have at the end of *The Quilter's Apprentice* is a dream and the desire to pursue it. That's a great beginning, but still, it is only a beginning. I thought it would be interesting to return to Sarah and Sylvia two years later to see if they were able to accomplish their goals. I also wondered if Sarah kept her promise to reconcile with her mother. The Sarah I knew was well-meaning but stubborn, and I thought this might create some conflict between her and Sylvia.

Secondly, I liked the friends Sarah met when she moved to Waterford—Gwen, Summer, Judy, Bonnie, Agnes, and Diane—and was eager for the chance to explore these characters more thoroughly. I wanted to learn about their goals, their dreams, the challenges they faced, and their perception of Elm Creek Manor. I especially wanted to uncover what had transpired at Elm Creek Manor during Sylvia's long absence; of all the surviving characters, only Agnes had witnessed those dark times, so I needed to be able to write from her point of view.

*Jennifer Chiaverini on the set of* Simply Quilts, *July 2001. Photo credit: Geraldine Neidenbach.*

*Nicholas Chiaverini helping his mother arrange the borders for the Challenge Quilt from* The Cross-Country Quilters. *Photo credit: Jennifer Chiaverini*

To my delight, *Round Robin* was also warmly received by readers eager to hear more about Elm Creek Manor. Quilters, especially, found the idea of quilt camp very appealing. Wherever my book tour took me, someone would invariably ask if Elm Creek Manor was a real place, and if so, how they could sign up for quilt camp. Unfortunately, while real quilt camps do exist, Elm Creek Quilt Camp does not.

I so regretted disappointing these eager, would-be campers that I decided to write a novel just for them, so they could experience the excitement and

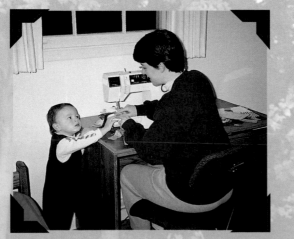

*Nicholas helping Jennifer sew together the signature blocks for the back of the Log Cabin quilt from* The Runaway Quilt. *Photo credit: Martin Chiaverini*

camaraderie of quilt camp through my characters' eyes. *The Cross-Country Quilters* features five women who attend camp at Elm Creek Manor and become fast friends despite their differences in age, race, and background. The novel traces their friendship as it is tested by time, distance, and conflict until they reunite the following year at Elm Creek Manor. *The Cross-Country Quilters* was both a special gift for true Elm Creek Quilts fans and a worthwhile challenge for me as a writer, to exercise my imagination by creating characters as rich and as real as the ones I already knew so well. To my delight, my readers embraced Donna, Megan, Grace, Julia, and Vinnie as warmly as they had the Elm Creek Quilters.

*The Runaway Quilt,* the fourth Elm Creek Quilts novel, allowed me to return Sylvia to center stage while also introducing new characters to the series. *The Runaway Quilt* is especially dear to me because I had wanted to tell this story for years—in fact, long before I even found a publisher for *The Quilter's Apprentice.*

My friend from the Internet Writing Workshop, Christine Johnson, inspired this book after she provided a critique of the eighth chapter of *The Quilter's Apprentice.* Upon reading the scene where Sylvia shows Sarah the gazebo and talks about the legend of the Log Cabin quilt with black center squares, Christine wondered what would have happened if someone had made such a quilt not realizing it was a secret signal, and inadvertently beckoned fugitive slaves to her home. I quickly recognized how potentially compelling and powerful such a story could be, so I tucked it away in a corner of my imagination, mulling it over in my subconscious until I felt I was ready to develop it into a story. The result, I believe, was worth the wait. *The Runaway Quilt* is my best work to date and is by far my favorite of the Elm Creek Quilts novels that exist as I write these words.

I hope I will feel that way about each Elm Creek Quilts novel I have yet to create.

Readers often tell me they want more stories about Sarah, Sylvia, and the Elm Creek Quilters, and I hope to be able to provide at least several more. When I do decide to move on to other subjects, I hope to bring my readers along on the journey. One thing is certain: Sarah, Sylvia, and the Elm Creek Quilters will always occupy a special place in my heart, but an even greater place is reserved for my readers, whose affection for my characters and enthusiastic support of my work never fail to inspire me.

In more recent years, I have also found inspiration in a particularly delightful source—my son, Nicholas. When he was just a few weeks old, Nicholas began accompanying me on my book tours, and as he grew older, he became more interested in meeting readers at book signings and playing with my fabric stash as I sewed the quilts from the stories. While it is not easy to juggle the demands of motherhood and a writing career, Marty has helped me achieve a healthy balance and Nicholas reminds me to keep my sense of humor in trying times. And of course, I feel a special burst of

*Nicholas and Marty sledding on the hill behind the Chiaverini home. January 2002. Photo credit: Jennifer Chiaverini*

pride when Nicholas tells me my quilts are pretty or points out copies of my novels in book stores and exclaims, "Look! Mama's book!" With such support from my family, I'm confident I will be able to keep writing for many years to come.

In the meantime, I invite you to try your hand at making one or more of the quilts that Sarah, Sylvia, and the Elm Creek Quilters made in my novels. A few other quilts designed by Nancy Odom were inspired by the characters or events: *Vinnie's Double Pinwheel, Andrew's Star in the Window,* or *When He Makes Dinner.* Honi Werner's cover art for *The Runaway Quilt* inspired *Joanna's Pumpkins and Pomegranates* quilt.

Many thanks to all of my loyal fans who found the time in their busy schedules to make a Log Cabin and signature block for *Gerda's Log Cabin* (see pages 76 and 79). I hope you are as pleased with the resulting two-sided quilt as I am.

Warm regards,

Jennifer

*Nicholas playing on the unquilted top of the crib-size* Birds in the Air *quilt from* The Runaway Quilt, *April 2002. Photo credit: Jennifer Chiaverini*

### Sylvia Compson

A gifted quilter, Sylvia Bergstrom Compson graduated with a degree in Art Education from Carnegie Mellon University in Pittsburgh. For many years she taught in the Sewickley, Pennsylvania area, but is known across the country as a fascinating and entertaining speaker and is a highly popular lecturer at quilt shows and quilt guilds. One of her quilts, *Sewickley Sunrise,* is a part of the permanent collection of the Museum of the American Quilter's Society in Paducah, Kentucky.

Sylvia considers herself a traditional quilter, but it would be more accurate to say she interprets traditional patterns in contemporary ways. Her favorite patterns are variations of the eight-pointed star, including the LeMoyne Star, Lone Star, Broken Star, Snow Crystals, and Carpenter's Wheel designs. She prefers jewel tones and tone-on-tone prints that read as solids, but she also enjoys challenging herself to work with fabrics that do not fit into her usual palette.

### Sarah McClure

While struggling to find a job in her new hometown of Waterford, Sarah works with Sylvia to prepare to sell Elm Creek Manor—the home Sylvia has returned to after a nearly fifty year absence. Quilting becomes the foundation for a blossoming friendship between the two women. Samplers become Sarah's favorite quilts to make because she enjoys learning to make each new block rather than making enough identical blocks for a whole quilt. Sarah's favorite color is blue, but she also likes earth tones, especially dusty reds and browns.

# The QUILTER'S APPRENTICE

The quilt from *The Quilter's Apprentice* needed to accomplish two tasks: It had to be a practical teaching tool for Sylvia's quilting lessons, and it needed to evoke memories from Sylvia's past in an effortless, realistic manner. The quilt's dual roles made designing *Sarah's Sampler* a unique challenge. I began by identifying sampler blocks that would increase in difficulty as the story progressed and would also teach Sarah different fundamental quilting skills. Of the many blocks that met these criteria, I chose those that flowed most naturally from a quilting lesson into one of Sylvia's stories. Sometimes I chose blocks because their names symbolized one of the book's themes— Hands All Around, for example, or Sister's Choice. On other occasions I knew what memory from Sylvia's past I wanted to depict and chose a block to best fit that scene; Little Red Schoolhouse and Double Nine-Patch were selected in this manner. More often, the block name appealed to me so much that I designed Sylvia's story around the block, such as when I chose Contrary Wife, Chimneys and Cornerstones, and Bachelor's Puzzle.

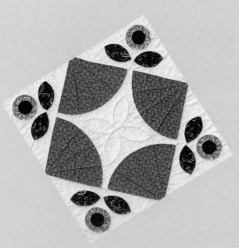

Machine pieced and hand quilted by Jennifer Chiaverini, 1998.

Finished Size: 80" x 96" (Double/Queen Bed Size)
Block Size: 12" x 12" finished
Number of Blocks: 12

# SARAH'S SAMPLER

## FABRIC REQUIREMENTS

**Light background:** 6½ yards (includes binding)

**Dark blue:** 2⅞ yards

**Medium blue:** 1½ yards

**Tan:** ⅜ yard

**Dark brown:** ⅜ yard

**Medium brown** (optional): ¼ yard

**Dark red:** ½ yard

**Medium red:** ⅝ yard

**Scrap of green** (optional for stems and leaves)

**Backing:** 7 yards

**Batting:** 84" x 100"

**Contrasting Binding** (optional): ¾ yard

**Fusible web** (optional): ½ yard

**Template plastic**

## SAWTOOTH STAR BLOCK

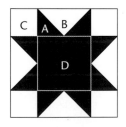

## Cutting

*Light background:* Cut one 3½"-wide strip. Cut the strip into four 3½" x 6½" rectangles (B), and four 3½" squares (C).

*Dark Blue:* Cut one 3½"-wide strip. Cut the strip into eight 3½" squares for star points (A).

Cut one 6½" square for star center (D).

## Block Assembly

**1.** Refer to Quilting 101, page 91, for making Flying Geese units for star points. Make 4 A/B units.

**2.** Sew the block together as shown. Press. The block should measure 12½" square.

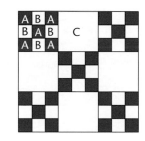

*Sawtooth Star Block Assembly*

## DOUBLE NINE-PATCH BLOCK

## Cutting

*Light background:* Cut two 1⅞"-wide strips, then cut the strips into four 1⅞" x 20" strips (B).

Cut four 4½" squares (C).

*Dark red:* Cut two 1⅞"-wide strips, then cut the strips into four 1⅞" x 20" strips (A).

## Block Assembly

**1.** Sew the strips together along the long edges to make one A/B/A strip set and one B/A/B strip set (one half strip of each will not be used).

Cut 10 A/B/A 1⅞" units and 5 B/A/B 1⅞" units.

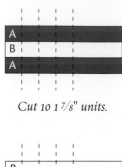

*Cut 10 1⅞" units.*

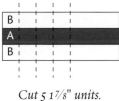

*Cut 5 1⅞" units.*

**3.** Sew the units together to make 5 Nine-Patch blocks. Press. Trim all blocks to 4½" square.

*Make 5.*

**4.** Sew the Nine-Patch blocks and squares (C) together into rows. Press.

**5.** Sew the rows together and press. The block should measure 12½".

*Double Nine-Patch Block Assembly*

## LITTLE RED SCHOOLHOUSE BLOCK

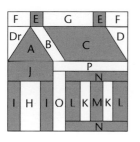

## Cutting

*Light background:* Cut 1 each of B, D, Dr using the Schoolhouse template patterns on page 25.

Cut two 2³/₄" x 2" rectangles (F).

Cut one 5¹/₂" x 2" rectangle (G).

Cut one 2¹/₂" x 5¹/₂" rectangle (H).

Cut two 1¹/₂" x 4¹/₂" rectangles (K).

Cut one 1³/₄" x 6¹/₂" rectangle (O).

Cut one 8" x 1¹/₂" rectangle (P).

*Medium red:* Cut 1 each of A and C each using Schoolhouse template patterns on pages 24 and 25.

Cut two 1³/₄" x 2" rectangles (E).

Cut two 1³/₄" x 5¹/₂" rectangles (I).

Cut one 5" x 2¹/₂" rectangle (J).

Cut two 2" x 4¹/₂" rectangles (L).

Cut one 1³/₄" x 4¹/₂" rectangle (M).

Cut two 6³/₄" x 1¹/₂" rectangles (N).

## Block Assembly

**1.** Sew the pieces together into a chimney/sky unit (E/F/G), a roof/sky unit (A/B/C/D), a door/house front unit (H/I/J), and a window/house side unit (K/L/M/N/O/P). Press.

**2.** Sew the units together to make the block. Press. The block should measure 12¹/₂" square.

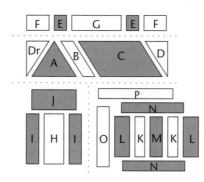

*Little Red Schoolhouse Block Assembly*

## CONTRARY WIFE BLOCK

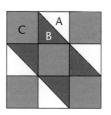

## Cutting

*Light:* Cut two 4⁷/₈" squares, then cut each square in half diagonally to make 4 half-square triangles (A).

*Medium red:* Cut one 4¹/₂"-wide strip, then cut the strip into five 4¹/₂" squares (C).

*Dark brown:* Cut two 4⁷/₈" squares, then cut each square in half diagonally to make 4 half-square triangles (B).

## Block Assembly

**1.** Make 4 half-square triangle units A/B. Press seam toward the dark triangle.

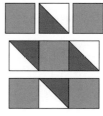

*Make 4.*

**2.** Sew A/B half-square triangle units and squares (C) together into rows. Press.

**3.** Sew the rows together and press. The block should measure 12¹/₂".

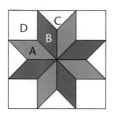

*Contrary Wife Block Assembly*

## LEMOYNE STAR BLOCK

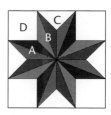

*LeMoyne Star Block*

*Note: Jennifer's block is a traditional LeMoyne Star block; Nancy's block splits each diamond in half.*

# Cutting

## Traditional Diamonds:

*Light background:* Cut one 6¼" square, then cut twice diagonally to make 4 quarter-square triangles (C).

Cut four 4" squares (D).

*Medium blue:* Cut 4 diamonds (A) using the LeMoyne Star template pattern A-B on page 24.

*Dark brown:* Cut 4 diamonds (B) using the LeMoyne Star template pattern A-B on page 24.

## Optional Split Diamonds:

*Medium blue:* Cut one 2½"-wide strip for star points (A).

*Dark blue:* Cut one 2½"-wide strip for star points (A).

Sew medium and dark blue strips together and press seam open. Center the LeMoyne Star template pattern A-B on page 24 over the seam and cut 4 diamonds (A).

*Star point A Cut 4*

*Medium brown:* Cut one 2½"-wide strip for star points (B).

*Dark brown:* Cut one 2½"-wide strip for star points (B).

Sew medium and dark brown strips together and press seam open. Center the diamond template over the seam and cut 4 diamonds (B).

---

*Star point B Cut 4*

# Block Assembly

**1.** Refer to Quilting 101, page 91, for Y-seam construction. Make 4 A/B/C units. Sew in the direction of the arrows, backstitching at the dot. Press toward the background piece (C).

*Make 4.*

**2.** Sew one A/B/C unit to square (D) backstitching at the dot. Press. Make 4 A/B/C/D units.

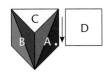

*Make 4.*

**3.** Sew together 2 A/B/C/D units to make half of the block. Sew in the direction of the arrows in the numbered order, backstitching at the dots. Press.

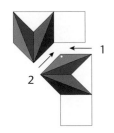

*Make 2 half-block units.*

---

**4.** Sew 2 halves together to complete the LeMoyne Star block. Sew the outer seams in the direction of the arrows, backstitching at each dot. Sew the center seams toward the arrows, starting and ending at each dot. Press. The block should measure 12½" square.

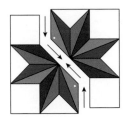

*Sew the 2 halves together.*

# BACHELOR'S PUZZLE BLOCK

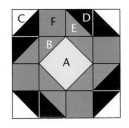

# Cutting

*Light background:* Cut two 3⅞" squares, then cut each square in half diagonally to make 4 half-square triangles (C).

*Tan:* Cut one 6½" square (A).

*Medium blue:* Cut four 3½" squares (B).

Cut two 3⅞" squares, then cut each square in half diagonally to make 4 half-square triangles (E).

*Medium red:* Cut four 3½" squares (F).

*Dark blue:* Cut four 3⅞" squares, then cut each square in half diagonally to make 8 half-square triangles (D).

## Block Assembly

**1.** To make the center square-in-a-square unit, sew 2 squares (B) onto opposite corners of the 6½" square (A). Trim the seams and press. Repeat for the remaining corners to complete the center A/B unit.

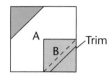

*Make one A/B unit.*

**2.** Make 4 C/D and 4 D/E half-square triangle units. Press seam toward the dark triangle.

*Make 4 units.*

*Make 4 units.*

**3.** Sew together 2 C/D units, a D/E unit and one square (F). Make 2 rows. Press.

**4.** Sew D/E unit and a square (F) to both sides of the center A/B square. Press.

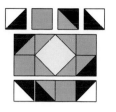

*Bachelor's Puzzle Block Assembly*

**5.** Sew the rows together. Press. The block should measure 12½" square.

## POSIES ROUND THE SQUARE BLOCK

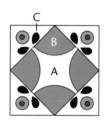

*Posies Round the Square Block*

## Cutting

Enlarge patterns 150%.

*Note: Nancy chose to add stems to the posies and to use green for the stems and leaves.*

*Light background:* Cut 1 center using Posies pattern A on page 26.

Cut two 6⅞" squares, then cut each square in half diagonally to make 4 half-square triangles (C).

*Medium blue:* Cut 4 quarter circles using Posies pattern B on page 26.

*Scraps:* Cut 4 flower centers, 4 posies, and 8 leaves using Posies template patterns on page 26.

## Block Assembly

**1.** Refer to Quilting 101, page 91, for curved seam piecing.

Pin a quarter-circle (B) to the center (A), matching the center points.

**2.** Sew the curved seam and press. Repeat for the other 4 corners to complete the center of the block.

**3.** Refer to Quilting 101, page 93, for preparation for appliqué. Appliqué the posies onto each of the 4 corner triangles (C) using your favorite method. For a folk art look, stitch the edges with a blanket stitch.

**4.** Sew the appliquéd triangle blocks (C) to the center block (A). Press.

The block should measure 12½" square.

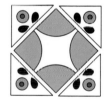

*Posy Block Assembly*

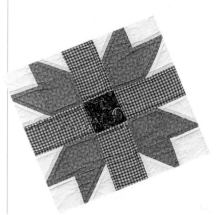

## LANCASTER ROSE BLOCK

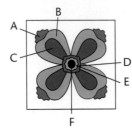

## Cutting

*Light background:* Cut one 13½" square.

*Scraps:* Cut 4 A, 4 B, 4 C, 1 D, 1 E, 1 F using Lancaster Rose template patterns A–F on page 26.

## Block Assembly

1. Refer to Quilting 101, page 93, for preparation for appliqué. Appliqué the shapes in alphabetical order onto the background square using your favorite method.

2. Press the appliquéd block. Trim the block to 12½" square.

## SISTER'S CHOICE BLOCK

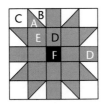

*Note: Nancy chose to cut 4 D from the light background and 4 D from dark blue.*

## Cutting

*Light:* Cut four 3⅜" squares, then cut each square in half diagonally to make 8 half-square triangles (B). Cut four 3" squares (C).

*Medium Red:* Cut eight 2½" rectangles (D).

*Medium blue:* Cut four 3⅜" squares, then cut each square in half diagonally to make 8 half-square triangles (A). Cut four 3" squares (E).

*Dark blue:* Cut one 2½" square (F).

## Block Assembly

1. Make 8 A/B units. Press seams toward darker fabric.

*Make 8 A/B units.*

2. Sew the A/B units with C, D, E, F into rows. Press.

3. Sew the rows together. Press. The block should measure 12½" square.

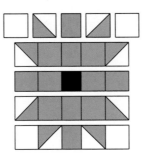

*Sister's Choice Block Assembly*

## HANDS ALL AROUND BLOCK

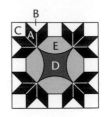

## Cutting

*Light background:* Cut 8 (B) using the Hands All Around template pattern B on page 27.

Cut 8 using Hands All Around template pattern C on page 27.

*Dark blue:* Cut 16 diamonds using the Hands All Around template pattern A on page 27.

*Dark red:* Cut 1 center using the Hands All Around template pattern D on page 27.

*Tan:* Cut 4 using the Hands All Around pattern template E on page 27.

## Block Assembly

1. Refer to Quilting 101, page 91, for Y-seam construction to make 8 A/B units.

*Make 8.*

**2.** Sew a square (C) to each A/B unit in the direction of the arrow. Backstitch at the dot. Press.

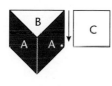

*Make 8.*

**3.** Sew 2 A/B/C units together to create an outer quarter of the block. Sew in the direction of the arrows, backstitching at the dot. Press.

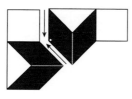

*Make 4.*

**4.** Refer to Quilting 101, page 91, for curved seam piecing to make the center D/E unit. Pin a curved piece (E) to center (D), matching center points. Sew the curved seam and press. Repeat for the other corners to complete the center of the block.

*Make 1.*

**5.** Sew the corner units to the center unit to complete the block. Sew the seams in the direction of the arrows, backstitching at each dot. Press. The block should measure 12½" square.

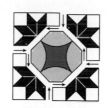

*Hands All Around Block Assembly*

## OHIO STAR BLOCK

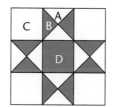

## Cutting

*Note: Nancy chose to use two different browns for B and D.*

**Light:** Cut two 5¼" squares, then cut each square twice diagonally into quarters to make 8 quarter-square triangles (A).

Cut four 4½" squares (C).

**Dark brown:** Cut two 5¼" squares, then cut each square into quarters diagonally to make 8 quarter-square triangles (B).

Cut one 4½" square (D).

## Block Assembly

**1.** Sew together 8 pairs of A and B triangles. Press. Then sew the pairs together to make 4 quarter-square triangle A/B units. Press.

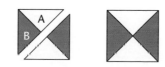

*Make 4.*

**2.** Sew the units together into rows. Press the seams toward the squares.

**3.** Sew the rows together. Press. The block should measure 12½" square.

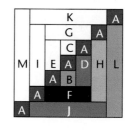

*Ohio Star Block Assembly*

## CHIMNEYS AND CORNERSTONES BLOCK

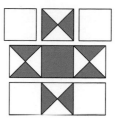

## Cutting

**Light background:** Cut one 2¼"-wide strip. From this strip cut one each:

2¼" x 2¼" (C)

2¼" x 4" (E)

2¼" x 5¾" (G)

2¼" x 7½" (I)

2¼" x 9¼" (K)

2¼" x 11" (M)

**Assorted mediums and darks:**
Cut one each:

2¼" x 2¼" (B)

2¼" x 4" (D)

2¼" x 5¾" (F)

2¼" x 7½" (H)

2¼" X 9¼" (J)

2¼" X 11" (L)

*Dark red:* Cut seven 2¼" squares (A).

## Block Assembly

1. Sew the corresponding corner-stones and chimneys into units.

2. Sew the units together as you would sew a Courthouse Steps block. The block should measure 12½" square. Trim if necessary.

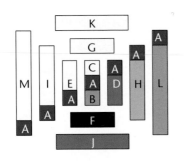

*Chimneys and Cornerstones Block Assembly*

## GARDEN MAZE SASHING

### Cutting

*Light background:* Cut two 12½"-wide strips. Cut these strips into thirty-one 2½" x 12½" rectangles for logs.

Cut three 2½"-wide strips. Cut these strips into seventy-two 1½" x 2½" rectangles (B) for Corner Posts and Stepping Stones.

Cut two 3⅞" squares, then cut each square in half diagonally (E) for Corner Posts.

*Dark blue:* Cut three 12½"-wide strips. Cut these strips into sixty-two 1½" x 12½" rectangles for logs.

Cut nine 1½"-wide strips. Cut these strips into 220–1½" squares total:

144 squares (A) for Stepping Stones and Corner Posts
64 squares (C) for Stepping Stones
12 squares (C) for Corner Posts

Cut one 2½"-wide strip, then cut the strip into sixteen 2½" squares (D) for Stepping Stones.

Cut two 3⅞" squares, then cut each square in half diagonally (F) for Corner Posts.

*Garden Maze Stepping Stone*

*Garden Maze Corner Post*

*Garden Maze Log*

### Sashing Assembly

1. To make the log units, sew a dark 1½" x 12½" rectangle to both sides of a light 2½" x 12½" rectangle. Press the seams toward the dark rectangles. Make 31 log units.

2. Refer to Quilting 101, page 91 to make 72 Flying Geese A/B units for the Stepping Stones and Corner Posts. Make 64 units for the Stepping Stones and 8 for the Corner Posts.

*Make 72 total.*

3. Sew each Stepping Stone block together as shown. Press. Make 16. The block should measure 4½" square.

*Stepping Stone Block Assembly*

4. Make 4 E/F half-square triangle units. Press toward the dark triangle.

*Make 4.*

5. Sew the Corner Posts together. Press. Make 4. The block should measure 4½" square.

*Corner Post Assembly*

*Jennifer Chiaverini on the set of* Simply Quilts. *Photo credit: Geraldine Neidenbach.*

## Block and Sashing Assembly

**1.** Sew the sampler blocks together with the sashing logs. Sew into rows. Press.

**2.** Sew sashing logs and stepping stones together to make each sashing row. Sew the corner posts at the ends of the top and bottom sashing rows. Press.

**3.** Sew the block and sashing rows together. Press.

## WIDE BORDER

### Cutting

*Light:* Cut eight 10½"-wide strips for the borders.

### Assembly

**1.** Sew strips end to end and cut two 10½" x 52½" strips for the side borders. Sew the borders to the sides of the quilt. Press the seams toward the border.

**2.** Sew strips end to end and cut two 10½" x 88½" strips for the top and bottom borders. Sew the borders to the top and bottom of the quilt. Press the seams toward the border.

## TWISTED RIBBON BORDER

### Cutting

*Light background:* Cut two 4⅞" squares, then cut in half diagonally to make 4 half-square triangles (A).

Cut three 5¼"-wide strips. Cut into twenty 5¼" squares, then cut each square twice diagonally into quarters to make 80 quarter-square triangles (C and F).

*Medium blue:* Cut six 4⅞"-wide strips. Cut the strips into forty-two 4⅞" squares, then cut each square in half diagonally to make 84 half-square triangles (B and E).

*Dark blue:* Cut three 5¼"-wide strips. Cut into twenty 5¼" squares, then cut each square twice diagonally into quarters to make 80 quarter-square triangles (D and G).

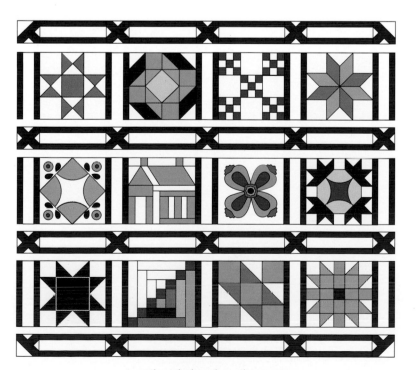

*Sampler Block and Garden Maze
Sashing Assembly*

## Assembly

**1.** Make 4 half-square triangle A/B corner units. Press toward the medium triangles.

*Make 4.*

**2.** Make 40 quarter-square triangle C/D units and 40 F/G units. Press toward the dark triangle.

*Note: The F/G unit is the reverse of the C/D unit.*

*Make 40.*     *Make 40.*

**3.** Sew a C/D unit to a triangle (E). Press seam toward E. Make 40 C/D/E units.

*Make 40.*

**4.** Sew an F/G unit to a triangle (E). Press seam toward E. Make 40 E/F/G units.

*Make 40.*

**5.** To make the side borders, sew 2 sets of 9 C/D/E units each and 2 sets of 9 E/F/G units each to make the strips used for the side borders. Press.

*9 C/D/E units*

*9 E/F/G units*

**6.** Sew a set of 9 C/D/E units to a set of 9 E/F/G units together end to end to make each border.

*Left border and right border*

**7.** Sew the borders to the sides of the quilt. Press the seams toward inner border.

*Note: The borders are sewn on as mirror images of each other.*

**8.** Sew 2 sets of 11 C/D/E units each and 2 sets of 11 E/F/G units each to make the strips needed for the top and bottom borders. Press.

*11 C/D/E units; make 2 sets.*

*11 E/F/G units; make 2 sets.*

**9.** Sew a set of 11 E/F/G units and a set of 11 C/D/E units to make each border. Make 2 as shown, one for the top border and one for the bottom border. Sew an A/B unit to each end.

*Top border and Bottom border*

**10.** Sew the borders to the top and bottom of the quilt. Press seams toward the inner border.

*Note: The borders are sewn on as mirror images of each other.*

**11.** Refer to Quilting 101, page 94, to layer the quilt top, batting, and backing; baste. Quilt as desired. Bind.

*Nancy Odom machine pieced and Melissa Taylor quilted this variation of Sarah's Sampler.*

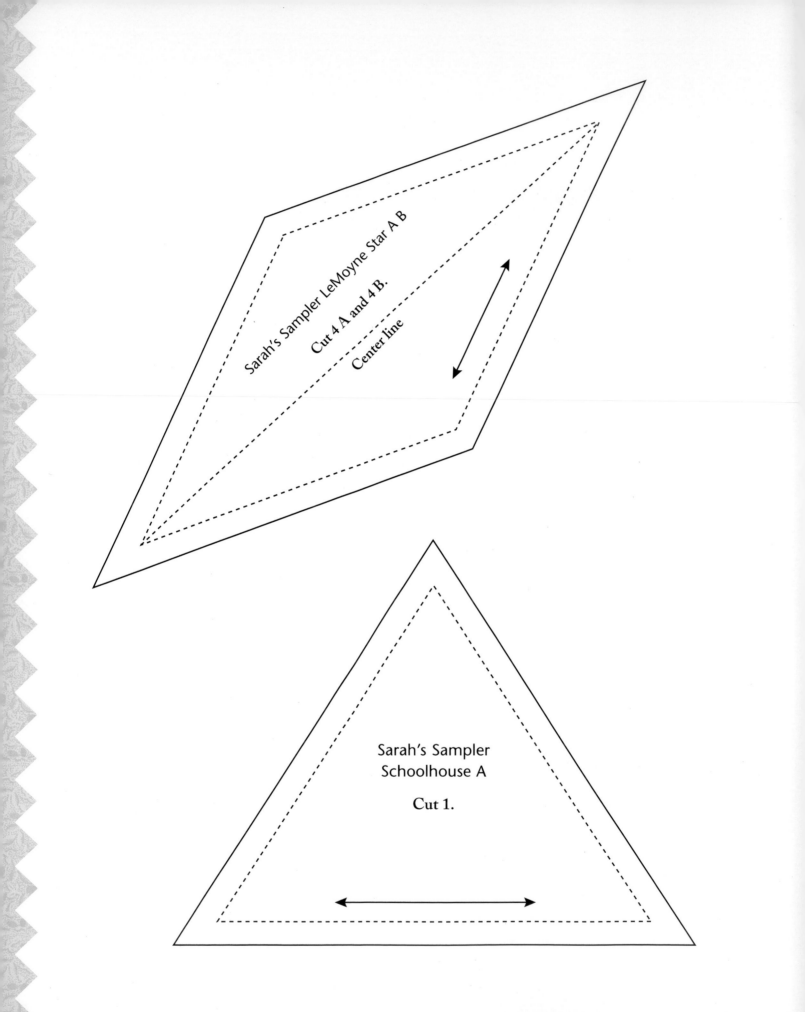

Sarah's Sampler LeMoyne Star A B

Cut 4 A and 4 B.

Center line

Sarah's Sampler
Schoolhouse A

Cut 1.

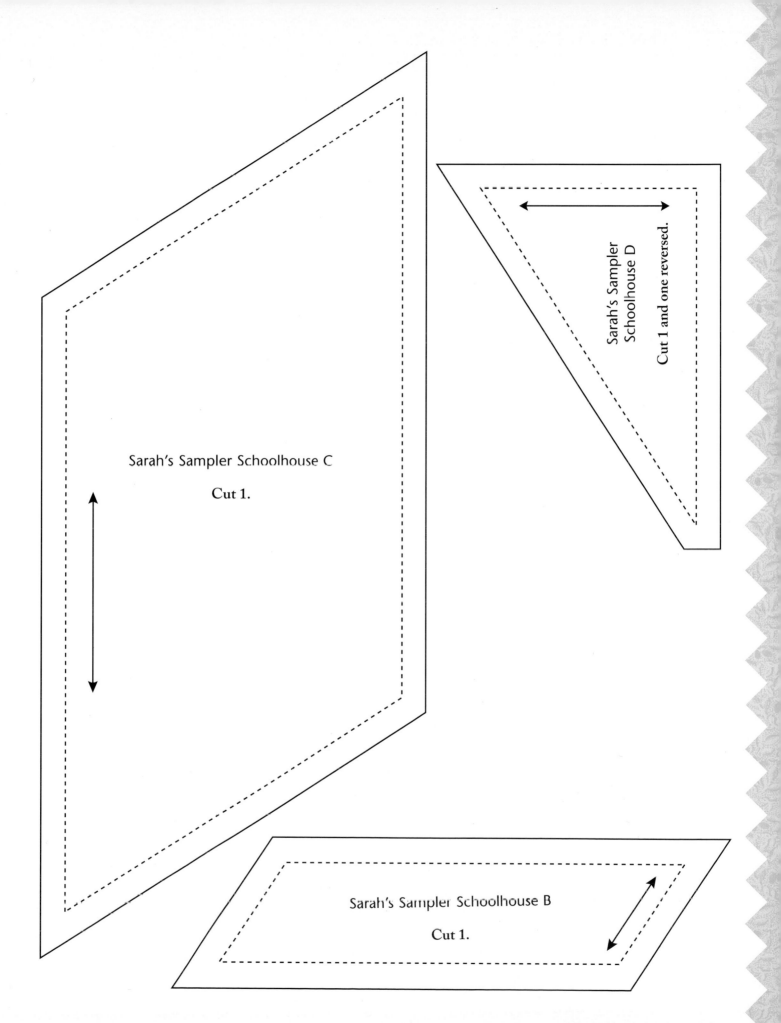

Sarah's Sampler Schoolhouse C

Cut 1.

Sarah's Sampler Schoolhouse D

Cut 1 and one reversed.

Sarah's Sampler Schoolhouse B

Cut 1.

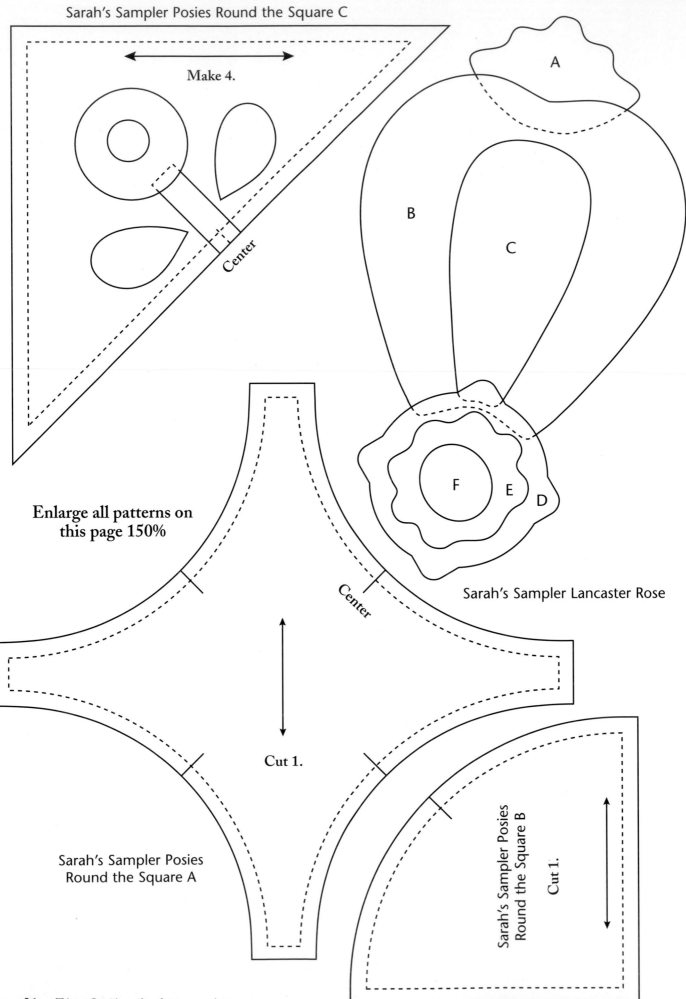

Sarah's Sampler Posies Round the Square C

Make 4.

Center

A

B

C

F E D

Enlarge all patterns on
this page 150%

Center

Sarah's Sampler Lancaster Rose

Cut 1.

Sarah's Sampler Posies
Round the Square A

Sarah's Sampler Posies
Round the Square B

Cut 1.

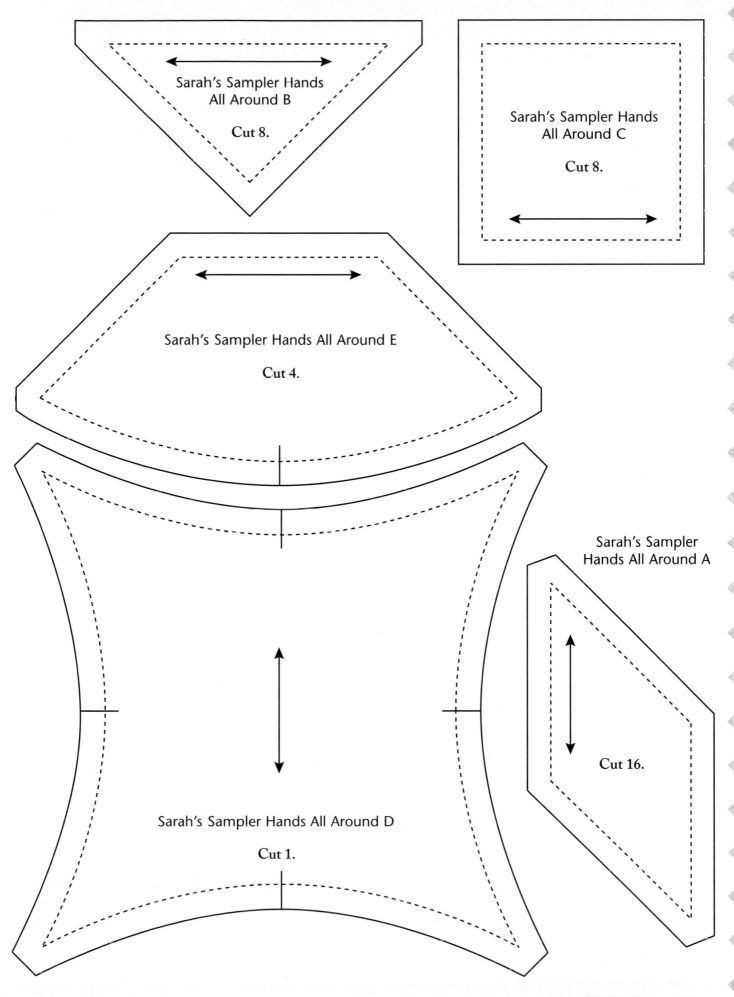

Sarah's Sampler Hands
All Around B

Cut 8.

Sarah's Sampler Hands
All Around C

Cut 8.

Sarah's Sampler Hands All Around E

Cut 4.

Sarah's Sampler
Hands All Around A

Cut 16.

Sarah's Sampler Hands All Around D

Cut 1.

# ROUND ROBIN

### Agnes Emberly

More than fifty years before their reunion in *Round Robin*, Agnes married Syvia's brother, Richard, against her parents' wishes. Estranged from her family, Agnes remained at Elm Creek Manor after Richard was killed in World War II. She later remarried, bore two daughters, and lived as a homemaker in Waterford, where she still resided when Sylvia returned after her long absence. An appliqué artist, Agnes prefers to work with small-scale calicoes.

### Diane Sonnenberg

The mother of two teenage boys and the wife of a Waterford College chemistry professor, Diane often finds herself exasperated and frenzied by the multiple demands of her career and family, but she is always the first to extend a hand to a friend in need. Diane is an adamant traditionalist, preferring hand piecing and hand quilting to machine work.

### Gwen Sullivan

A professor of American Studies, colorful, free-spirited Gwen is a self-proclaimed "former hippie" who sees quilting as a feminist act as well as a fulfilling art. A longtime single mother, Gwen enjoys a close, loving relationship with her daughter, Summer. She prefers vibrant colors, quirky patterns, and unusual techniques, such as photo transfer and hand dying.

### Summer Sullivan

A graduate of Waterford College majoring in philosophy, Summer Sullivan is the co-director of Elm Creek Quilt Camp. The youngest of the Elm Creek Quilters, Summer is fascinated by quilts as cultural and historical artifacts, and blends contemporary patterns and techniques with traditional fabrics.

### Judy Nguyen DiNardo

The daughter of an American serviceman and a Vietnamese woman, Judy immigrates to the United States as a young child, but she does not meet her biological father until she is in her thirties. A professor of computer sciences, Judy enjoys an affectionate marriage and is devoted to her young daughter, Emily. Judy prefers hand piecing and quilting, because she finds it relaxing after putting in long hours with her computers.

In *Round Robin*, wherein Sarah and her friends create a group quilt to hang in the foyer of Elm Creek Manor as a gift for Sylvia, I faced a very different creative challenge. Whereas in *The Quilter's Apprentice* I needed a device to inspire Sylvia's reminiscences, in my second novel I wanted to find a way to narrate stories from the perspectives of several different characters. After considering several ideas, I decided to use a Round Robin quilt, a quilt created by sewing concentric patchwork borders to a central block as it is passed around a circle of friends. As each woman adds her border to the quilt, she becomes the narrator of the story, and thus her past, her dreams, her struggles, and her triumphs are revealed. Appropriately, each woman draws inspiration from her own life when she designs her contribution to the quilt. I chose *Round Robin* as the title for the novel both to recognize the *Elm Creek Medallion* and also to symbolize the motion of the storytelling, as the focus shifts from one Elm Creek Quilter to the next as the quilt is passed from friend to friend.

Nancy Odom's design for *Andrew's Star in the Window* was inspired by Andrew's developing relationship with Sylvia. The fabric, a cozy flannel that matches Andrew's warm personality, celebrates his love of fishing.

*Sylvia's Broken Star* was loosely based on the quilt Sylvia works on after she suffers a stroke. With characteristic determination, Sylvia works on the quilt as part of her rehabilitation, and refuses to cave in to her physical limitations.

*When He Makes Dinner* is Craig's peace offering to Bonnie after she discovers and thwarts his plans to rendezvous with a woman he met on the Internet. The Broken Dishes blocks in the design are appropriate; most women in Bonnie's situation would be tempted to hurl a few dishes at their husbands!

Machine pieced and quilted by Jennifer Chiaverini, 2000.

Finished Size: 72¹/₂" x 72¹/₂"

# ELM CREEK MEDALLION

## FABRIC REQUIREMENTS

*Note: Two options for the center medal-lion are offered: the manor pictured in Jennifer's quilt, or a paper-pieced Mariner's Compass (see page 33).*

**Light background:** 3³/₄ yards

**Blues to total:** 1 yard

**Greens to total:** 1 yard

**Golds to total:** 1 yard

**Grays and blacks to total:** 1 yard

## MANOR CENTER MEDALLION OPTION:

**Sky Blue and Grass Green:** ¹/₃ yard each

**Light yellow, medium and dark gray, brown, and six different greens:** ¹/₈ yard each

**Light gray:** ¹/₄ yard

## MARINER'S COMPASS CENTER MEDALLION OPTION:

**Two golds, two blues, and two greens:** ¹/₄ yard each

**Backing:** 4¹/₃ yards

**Batting:** 77" x 77"

**Binding:** ⁵/₈ yard

**Template plastic** (optional)

**Fusible paper-backed adhesive** (optional): 2¹/₄ yards

## MANOR APPLIQUÉ MEDALLION OPTION:

### Cutting

**Light background:** Cut one 20" square.

Appliqué Fabrics:
(See page 35 for color placement.) Use green grass print for the grass (1) and light blue sky print for the sky (2). Use various green scraps for the mountains and three tops (3, 4, 5 6, 7, 8), and brown for the tree trunks (9, 10). Use light gray for the manor front, porch and steps (11, 12, 15, 15R). Use medium gray for the porch and roof edges (13, 13R, 14R). Use dark gray for the roof, pillars, door, and stair edge (16, 17, 18, 19). Use light yellow for the windows (20, 21, 22, 23).

### Assembly

1. Refer to Quilting 101, page 93, for appliqué preparation and instructions. The template pattern for the appliqué block is on page 35. Enlarge the pattern 400% before making the templates.

2. Appliqué the shapes using your favorite method following the numerical order on the diagram.

3. Appliqué the completed center onto the 20" background square. Press. Trim block to 18¹/₂" square.

## MARINER'S MEDALLION CENTER OPTION:

### Assembly

1. Refer to Quilting 101, page 92, for paper-piecing instructions. Enlarge the Mariner's Compass patterns A and B 135%, pages 34 and 35. Make 4 copies of each pattern.

2. Paper piece each Mariner's Compass section. For Section A use a light background, light green, light blue, dark blue, and light gold. For Section B use light background, dark green, light blue, dark blue, and dark gold.

*Section A*

*Section B*

3. Sew the 8 sections together, alternating A and B.

4. Remove the paper from the back and trim the center medallion to 18½" square (includes the seam allowance).

## FIRST BORDER: SQUARES ON POINT

### Cutting

*Light background:* Cut two 3¼"-wide strips, then cut the strips into eighteen 3¼" squares. Cut each square twice diagonally into quarters to make 72 quarter-square triangles (B).

Cut one 1½"-wide strip, then cut into eight 1½" squares. Cut each square in half diagonally to make 16 half-square triangles (C).

*From assorted blues:* Cut twenty 1⅞" squares (A).

*From assorted greens:* Cut twenty 1⅞" squares (A).

### Assembly

*Note: For ease in cutting and piecing, we used fewer squares in the first border than are shown in the quilt photo.*

1. To make each border unit, sew 2 triangles (B) to a square (A). Press seams toward the square. Make 32 A/B blocks.

*Make 32.*

2. To make each border end unit, sew 2 triangles (C) and one triangle (B) to a square (A). Press seams toward the square. Make 8 A/B/C units.

*Make 8.*

3. Sew 7 A/B units and 2 A/B/C units together to make each top and bottom border.

*Top and Bottom Border*

4. Sew 9 A/B units and 2 A/B/C units together to make each side border.

*Side Border*

5. If necessary, trim the center medallion block to fit the first border.

6. Sew the top and bottom borders, then the side borders, to the center square. Press seams toward the center medallion.

## SETTING TRIANGLES

### Cutting

*Light Background:* Cut two 16⅞" squares, then cut each square in half diagonally to make 4 half-square triangles.

## QUILT ASSEMBLY

Sew the 2 setting triangles to the sides of the quilt top, matching the center of the triangle to the center of the block. Press the seams toward the triangles. Repeat to add the other two setting triangles.

*Note: The triangle edges will be slightly larger than the sides of the quilt top.*

*Add setting triangles.*

## SECOND BORDER: PINWHEEL BLOCKS

*Note: For ease in cutting and piecing, we used fewer pinwheel blocks in the second border than are shown in the quilt photo.*

### Cutting

*Light background:* Cut six 2⅞"-wide strips, then cut the strips into seventy-two 2⅞" squares. Cut each square in half diagonally to make 144 half-square triangles (A).

**Blue:** Cut two 2⅞"-wide strips, then cut the strips into twenty-four 2⅞" squares. Cut each square in half diagonally to make 48 half-square triangles (B).

**Green:** Cut two 2⅞"-wide strips, then cut the strips into twenty-four 2⅞" squares. Cut each square in half diagonally to make 48 half-square triangles (B).

**Gold:** Cut two 2⅞"-wide strips, then cut the strips into twenty-four 2⅞" squares. Cut each square in half diagonally to make 48 half-square triangles (B).

*Note: For a scrappy look, cut the squares from several blue, green, and gold fabrics.*

## Assembly

1. Make 48 pairs of each color combination. Press toward the darker triangle.

*Make 48 of each color.*

2. Sew 4 triangles of the same color together to make one pinwheel block. Press.

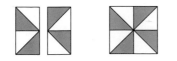

*Make 12 of each color.*

3. To make each side pinwheel border, sew 8 pinwheel blocks together. Press. Make 2. Sew the borders to the quilt top. Press toward the setting triangles.

4. To make the top and bottom borders, sew 10 pinwheel blocks together. Press. Make 2. Sew the borders to the quilt top. Press toward the setting triangles.

## HALF MARINER'S COMPASS BLOCKS

### Cutting

Cut the fabric pieces slightly larger than the size of the corresponding paper-pattern piece. Use the quilt photo as a guide for selecting colors.

### Assembly

1. Refer to Quilting 101, page 92, for paper-piecing instructions. Enlarge Mariner's Compass patterns A and B 200%, pages 34 and 35. Make 8 copies of each pattern.

2. Paper piece the Mariner's Compass section. For Section A use light background, dark gold, light blue, light gray, and dark gray. For Section B use light background, light gold, dark blue, light gray, and dark gray as shown.

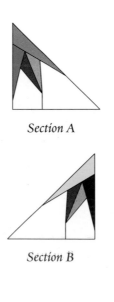

*Section A*

*Section B*

3. Refer to the photo for placement and sew 2 A sections and 2 B sections together to make one half Mariner's Compass triangle. Remove the paper backing.

4. Measure and trim the Mariner's Compass triangles if necessary to fit the quilt top.

5. Sew the corners to the quilt top.

## OUTER BORDER: CRAZY PATCH BLOCKS

### Cutting

Cut the fabric scraps slightly larger than the size of the corresponding paper pattern piece. Use the quilt photo as a guide to selecting colors.

### Crazy Patch Border Assembly

1. Refer to Quilting 101, page 92, for paper piecing instructions.

2. Enlarge the paper-piecing pattern for the Crazy Patch border 200%, page 34, and make 36 copies. Paper piece the 36 Crazy Patch blocks.

3. Sew together 8 blocks for each side border. Make 2. Sew to the sides of the quilt. Press.

4. Sew together 10 blocks each for the top and bottom borders. Make 2. Sew the borders to the top and bottom of the quilt. Press toward the Mariner's Compass.

5. Refer to Quilting 101, page 94, to layer the quilt top, batting, and backing; baste. Quilt as desired. Bind.

*Quilt Assembly Diagram with*
*Elm Creek Manor Center Medallion*

*Quilt Assembly Diagram with Mariner's Compass Center*

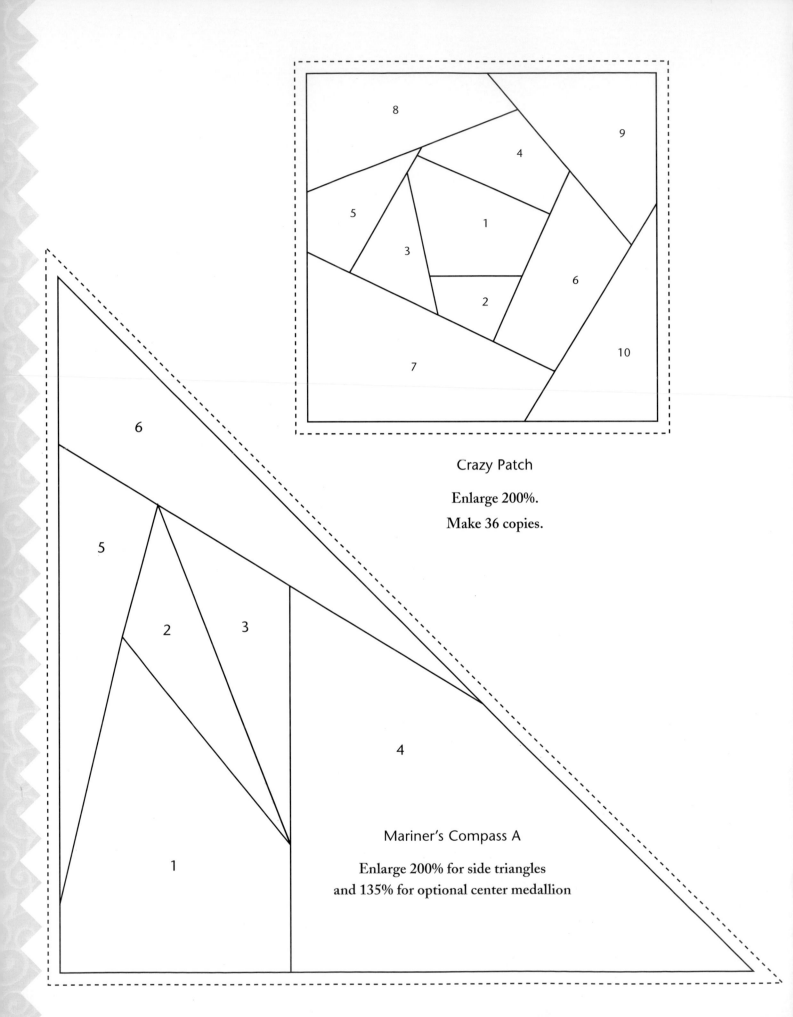

Crazy Patch

Enlarge 200%.

Make 36 copies.

Mariner's Compass A

Enlarge 200% for side triangles
and 135% for optional center medallion

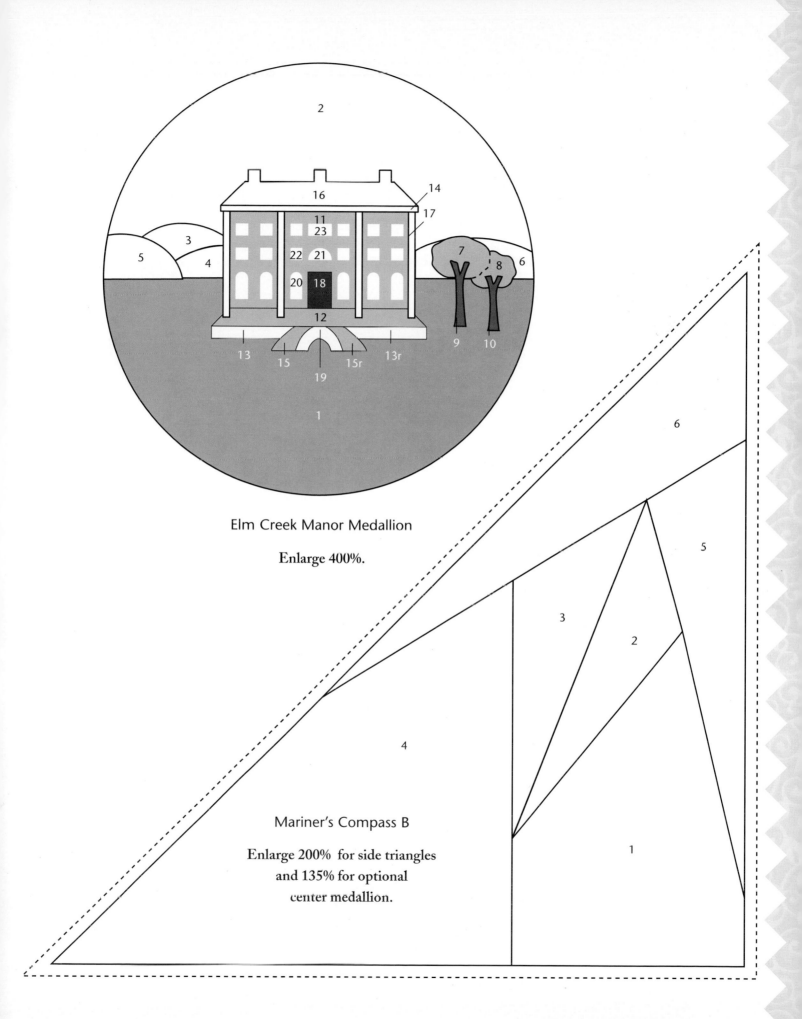

Elm Creek Manor Medallion

Enlarge 400%.

Mariner's Compass B

Enlarge 200% for side triangles
and 135% for optional
center medallion.

Machine pieced and quilted by Nancy Odom, 2002.
*Fabrics for this quilt were generously donated by RJR Fashion Fabrics.*

Finished Size: 43" x 43"
Block Size: 9¹/₂" finished
Number of Blocks: 5, with 4 corner blocks

# SYLVIA'S
# BROKEN STAR

## FABRIC REQUIREMENTS

**White:** 1¼ yard (includes inner border)

**Light red-violet:** ⅛ yard

**Red-violet:** 1⅛ yards (includes outer border)

**Blue:** ⅞ yard (includes binding)

**Light blue:** ½ yard

**Green:** ⅛ yard

**Light green:** ½ yard (includes middle border)

**Backing:** 2¾ yards

**Batting:** 48" x 48"

## Cutting

Copy Sylvia's Broken Star template patterns A and C on page 41.

*White:* Cut four 2"-wide strips for the inner border.

Cut one 10"-wide strip. Cut the strip into four 10" squares for alternate blocks.

Cut one 3¾"-wide strip. Cut the strip into five 3¾" squares, then cut each square twice diagonally into quarters to make 20 quarter-square triangles (B).

Cut three 1¾"-wide strips. Use Sylvia's Broken Star half-trapezoid pattern C to cut 20 left half-trapezoids and 20 right half-trapezoids.

**Tip:**

*To simplify cutting of these mirror-image pieces, place the strips wrong sides together and cut 20 left trapezoids. The bottom strip will automatically be cut into the right trapezoids.*

Cut two 2¾"-wide strips, then cut the strips into twenty 2¾" squares (D).

*Red-violet:* Use Sylvia's Broken Star Diamond pattern A to cut 8 diamonds.

Cut two 3¾" squares, then cut each square twice diagonally into quarters to make 8 quarter-square triangles (B) for the Broken Star border corners.

Cut four 3⅛" squares, then cut each square in half diagonally to make 8 half-square triangles (E) for the Broken Star border corners.

Cut four 2¾" squares (D) for the Broken Star border corners.

Cut one 1¾"-wide strip. Use pattern C to cut 8 left half-trapezoids and 8 right half-trapezoids for the Broken Star border corner. See Tip above for cutting.

Cut four 5¼"-wide strips for the outer border.

*Light red-violet:* Use diamond pattern A to cut 16 diamonds.

*Blue:* Use diamond pattern A to cut 16 diamonds for the Star blocks and 16 diamonds for the Broken Star border corners.

*Light blue:* Use diamond pattern A to cut 32 diamonds for the Star blocks

and 32 for the Broken Star border corners.

*Green:* Use diamond pattern A to cut 16 diamonds.

*Light green:* Use diamond pattern A to cut 32 diamonds for the star blocks.

Cut four 1½"-wide strips for the middle borders.

## Block Assembly

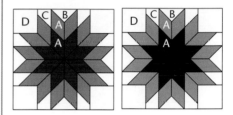

*Blocks A and B Make 1 each.*

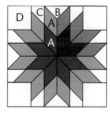

*Block C Make 1.*

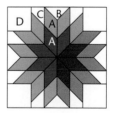

*Block D Make 1.*

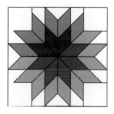

*Block E Make 1.*

Note: *Follow the diagrams on page 37 for color placement in each star, particularly Blocks C, D and E, which use 2 colorways.*

**1.** Refer to Quilting 101, page 91, for Y-seam construction. For each Star block use 8 dark diamonds (A), 16 light diamonds (A), 4 white triangles (B), 8 white half-trapezoids (C), and 4 white squares (D). Press.

**2.** Sew a light diamond (A) to a dark diamond (A).

**3.** Sew a light (A) and dark (A) pair together to make a mirror image. Press.

**4.** Sew the mirror image A/A units together. Press carefully.

Note: *For Blocks C and D you will make 2 units using both blue and green.*

*Make 6 green, 6 blue, and 4 red-violet.*

*Make 2.*

*Make 2.*

**5.** Using Y-seam construction, sew an A/A diamond unit to a white triangle (B), backstitching at the dot. Press.

*Make 16 one color pairs total.*

*Make 2.*

*Make 2.*

**6.** Sew a light diamond (A) to a right half-trapezoid (C), and sew a second light diamond (A) to a left half-trapezoid (Cr). Press.

**7.** Sew the mirror-image A/C units together, backstitching at the dot.

Note: *For Block D and E you will make 1 blue A/C unit, 2 green A/C units, and 1 A/C unit with both blue and green. Refer to the block diagrams on page 37 to help put the mirror-image A/C units together.*

*Make 7 green, 7 blue, and 4 red-violet.*

*Make 1 for Block D.*

*Make 1 for Block E.*

**8.** Using Y-seam construction, sew the right and left A/C units to a square (D), backstitching at the dot. Press.

*Make 7 green, 7 blue, and 4 red-violet.*

*Make 1.*

*Make 1.*

**9.** Sew 1 A/C/D unit to 1 A/B unit. Refer to the block diagrams on page 37 to note the color placement of the units. Press.

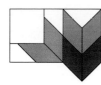

*Make 4 green, 4 blue, and 4 red-violet.*

*Make 2.*

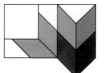

*Make 2.*

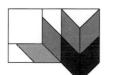

*Make 1 for Block D.*

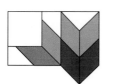

*Make 1 for Block E.*

**10.** Sew 4 units together to complete the block. Sew in the direction of the arrows and backstitch at the dots. Refer to the star diagrams on page 37 for A/B/C/D unit placement. Press.

*Block Assembly*

## HALF BROKEN STAR BORDER CORNER BLOCK ASSEMBLY

For each Half Broken Star block you will need 4 blue diamonds (A), 8 light blue diamonds (A), 2 red-violet quarter-square triangles (B), 4 red-violet half-trapezoids (C), 1 red-violet square (D), and 2 red-violet half-square triangles (E). Make 4 half Broken Star corner blocks.

**1.** Follow Steps 1–9 of the block assembly on pages 38-39. Substitute red-violet B, C, and D for the white pieces in the center block. Make 2 A/B units and 1 A/C/D unit for each corner block.

**2.** For each block sew a diamond (A) to a right half-trapezoid (C) and a triangle (E). Sew a diamond (A) to a left half-trapezoid (Cr) and a triangle (E). Press.

*Make 1.*

*Make 1.*

**3.** Sew A/B, A/C/D, and A/C/E units together to make half Broken Star corner blocks. Sew in the direction of the arrows, backstitching at the dots. Make 4. Press.

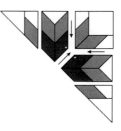

*Block Assembly*

## QUILT ASSEMBLY

**1.** Sew the star blocks and white alternate blocks together into rows. Press the seams of alternating rows in opposite directions.

**2.** Sew the rows together and press.

**3.** Refer to Quilting 101, page 93, for adding borders. Cut two 2" x 29" side inner border strips and two 2" x 32" top and bottom inner borders from the 2"-wide white strips. Sew the borders to the sides and then the top and bottom of the quilt top. Press the seams toward the borders.

**4.** Cut two 1½" x 32" side middle borders and two 1½" x 34" top and bottom middle borders from the 1½"-wide light green strips. Sew to the sides and then the top and bottom of the quilt top. Press the seams toward the middle borders.

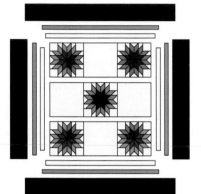

**5.** Cut two 5¼" x 34" side outer borders and two 5¼" x 43½" top and bottom outer borders from the 5¼"-wide red-violet strips, sewing end to end as necessary. Sew the borders to the sides and then the top and bottom of the quilt top. Press the seams toward the outer borders.

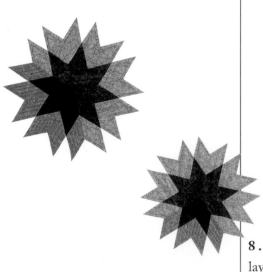

**6.** Prepare to add the half Broken Star corner blocks by trimming each corner of the outer border at a 45° angle. Be sure to trim ¼" outside each corner of the green middle border to retain a seam allowance for sewing on the corner block.

Trim to ¼" seam allowance.

*Trim quilt corners.*

**7.** Sew the Half Broken Star border blocks to the corners of the quilt top. Press.

*Quilting detail*

*Quilt Assembly Diagram*

**8.** Refer to Quilting 101, page 94, to layer the quilt top, batting, and backing; baste. Quilt as desired. Bind.

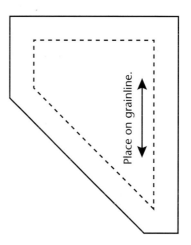

**Sylvia's Broken Star
Half-Trapezoid C**

Cut 20 and 20 reversed
white and cut 8 and 8
reversed red-violet.

Place on grainline.

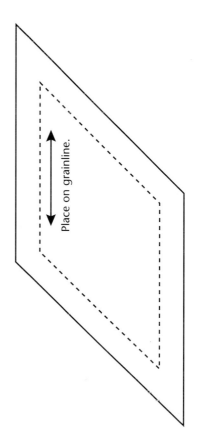

*Sylvia had made other quilts like it, but although these points were not as sharp as usual, nor the quilting stitches so fine and straight, she was prouder of this quilt than any other she had ever made. This quilt was a testament not to her skills but to her courage, to her refusal to give up. She had hoped that her friends would understand that, because she wanted them to know what it would mean to her when this quilt hung in the foyer and welcomed their guests to Elm Creek Manor. She hoped her friends did not need her to explain, because what she had put into that quilt she did not think she could put into words.*

Excerpted from *Round Robin*
by Jennifer Chiaverini

Place on grainline.

**Sylvia's Broken Star Diamond A**

Machine pieced by Nancy Odom, machine quilted by Marilyn at the Back Door Quilt Shop, Greenwood, IN, 2002.

*Fabrics for this project were generously donated by Moda Fabrics.*

Finished Size: 72" x 88"
Block Size: 16" finished (8" Star with sashing)
Number of Blocks: 20

# ANDREW'S STAR IN THE WINDOW

## FABRIC REQUIREMENTS

**Green:** 1³/₈ yards

**Dark green:** 3¹/₈ yards (includes border and binding)

**Gold:** 1 yard

**Red:** 1 yard

**Tan 1:** 1⁵/₈ yards

**Tan 2:** 1⁵/₈ yards

**Backing:** 5¹/₄ yards

**Batting:** 76" x 92"

## Cutting

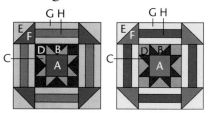

*Green:* Cut two 4¹/₂"-wide strips, then cut the strips into ten 4¹/₂" squares (A).

Cut three 4⁷/₈"-wide strips, then cut into twenty 4⁷/₈" squares. Cut each square in half diagonally to make 40 half-square triangles (F).

Cut two 8¹/₂"-wide strips, then cut the strips into forty 2" x 8¹/₂" rectangles (H).

*Dark green:* Cut two 4¹/₂"-wide strips, then cut the strips into ten 4¹/₂" squares (A).

Cut three 4⁷/₈"-wide strips, then cut into twenty 4⁷/₈" squares. Cut each square in half diagonally to make 40 half-square triangles (F).

Cut two 8¹/₂"-wide strips, then cut into forty 2" x 8¹/₂" rectangles (H).

Cut nine 4¹/₂"-wide strips for the borders.

*Gold:* Cut five 2¹/₂"-wide strips, then cut the strips into forty 4¹/₂" x 2¹/₂" rectangles (B).

Cut eight 2¹/₂"-wide strips, then cut the strips into forty 2¹/₂" squares (D) and eighty 2¹/₂" squares (C).

*Red:* Cut five 2¹/₂"-wide strips, then cut the strips into forty 4¹/₂" x 2¹/₂" rectangles (B).

Cut eight 2¹/₂"-wide strips, then cut the strips into forty 2¹/₂" squares (D) and eighty 2¹/₂" squares (C).

*Tan 1:* Cut three 4⁷/₈"-wide strips, then cut the strips into twenty 4⁷/₈" squares. Cut each square in half diagonally to make 40 half-square triangles (E).

Cut four 8¹/₂"-wide strips, then cut into eighty 1³/₄" x 8¹/₂" rectangles (G).

*Tan 2:* Cut three 4⁷/₈"-wide strips, then cut the strips into twenty 4⁷/₈" squares. Cut each square in half diagonally to make 40 half-square triangles (E).

Cut four 8¹/₂"-wide strips, then cut into eighty 1³/₄" x 8¹/₂" rectangles (G).

## Andrew Cooper

Andrew Cooper has admired Sylvia from the time he was her younger brother's boyhood friend. When Andrew and Sylvia reunited after a long separation, their friendship soon grew into mutual affection, and then blossomed into love. He asked Sylvia several times to marry him before she finally agreed, moved by revelations from the journal of her great-grandfather's sister, Gerda Bergstrom, not to let love pass her by.

Andrew enjoys the outdoors and travel, and his favorite pastime is fishing. While he has never made a quilt, he understands and appreciates all the time, energy, and creativity that goes into each project. He is proud of Sylvia's accomplishments and supports her in any way he can, including carrying her bags at quilt shows so she can purchase more fabric.

## Block Assembly

**1.** Refer to Quilting 101, page 91, to make the B/C Flying Geese units. Make B/C Flying Geese units in each of the 2 colorways, 4 for each of the 10 blocks.

*Make 40.*     *Make 40.*

**2.** Sew the Flying Geese B/C units to squares A and D to make the star. Press. Make 10 stars of each colorway.

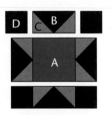

*Make 10.*

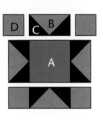

*Make 10.*

**3.** Make E/F units in each of the 2 colorways, 4 for each of the 10 blocks. Press the seam toward the darker fabric.

*Make 40.*     *Make 40.*

**4.** Sew one rectangle (H) between two rectangles (G). Press seams toward the center rectangle. Make G/H units in each of the 2 colorways, 4 for each of the 10 blocks.

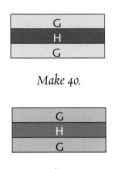

*Make 40.*

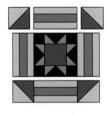

*Make 40.*

**5.** Sew the E/F units, G/H units, and Sawtooth Stars together into blocks. Press. Make 10 blocks of each colorway.

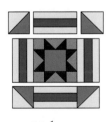

*Make 10.*

*Make 10.*

## QUILT ASSEMBLY

**1.** Alternating colorway 1 with colorway 2, sew blocks together into rows. Press the seams of alternating rows in opposite directions.

**2.** Sew the rows together. Press.

**3.** Refer to Quilting 101, page 93, for adding borders. Sew border strips end to end and cut two 4½" x 80½" side borders. Sew to both sides of the quilt top. Press the seams toward the border.

**4.** Sew strips end to end and cut 4½" x 72½" top and bottom borders. Sew to the top and bottom of the quilt top. Press the seams toward the border.

**5.** Refer to Quilting 101, page 94, to layer the quilt top, batting, and backing; baste. Quilt as desired. Bind.

*Quilt Assembly Diagram*

> *A*gnes reached over and took her hand.
> "Sylvia, Andrew will stay if you ask him to."
> "I couldn't possibly."
> "He wants you to."
> For a moment Sylvia was too startled to speak. "I couldn't. I couldn't impose on him like that. I can't have him staying on because he feels sorry for me."
> "That isn't how he feels, and that's not why he'd stay."
> Sylvia hesitated, then nodded. For several weeks now, she had been unable to ignore her growing affection for Andrew. Ever since he had sat on the edge of her bed and helped her remember how to quilt, she had known his heart as plainly as her own. It was nonsense, she had told herself, for a woman her age to be falling in love—but that was not what had held her back.
>
> Excerpted from *Round Robin*
> by Jennifer Chiaverini

Machine pieced by Cyndy Lyle Rymer, appliqué blocks by Joyce Lytle;
machine quilted by Linda Leathersich, 2002.

*Fabrics for this quilt were graciously donated by Moda Fabrics.*

Finished Size: 46½" x 46½"
Block Size: 10" finished
Number of Blocks: 4 appliquéd and 5 Large Broken Dishes blocks for center,
and 32 Small Broken Dishes Blocks for the border

# WHEN HE MAKES DINNER

## FABRIC REQUIREMENTS

**Background:** 1⅞ yards

**Tan:** ¼ yard

**Green 1:** ⅞ yard (includes outer border and binding)

**Greens 2 and 3:** ¼ yard each

**Blue 1:** ½ yard

**Blue 2:** ⅓ yard

**Red 1:** ¾ yard (includes inner border)

**Red 2:** ¼ yard

**Gold 1:** ⅓ yard

**Gold 2:** ¼ yard

**Backing:** 3 yards

**Batting:** 51" x 51"

**Template plastic**

**Fusible paper-backed adhesive** (optional)

## Cutting

*Large Broken Dishes Block*

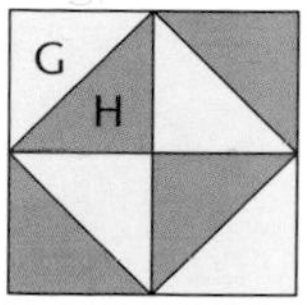

*Small Broken Dishes Block*

*Background:* Cut four 14" squares for the appliquéd blocks. The blocks will be trimmed to 10½" square when the appliqué is completed.

Cut two 2½"-wide strips, then cut the strips into twenty 2½" squares (A).

Cut two 2⅞"-wide strips, then cut the strips into twenty 2⅞" squares. Cut each square in half diagonally to make 40 half-square triangles (B).

Cut six 3⅜"-wide strips, then cut the strips into sixty-four 3⅜" squares. Cut each square in half diagonally to make 128 half-square triangles (G).

*Tan:* Cut one 3⅞"-wide strip then cut the strip into ten 3⅞" squares. Cut each square in half diagonally to make 20 half-square triangles (F).

*Green 1:* Cut five 1¼"-wide strips for the outer borders.

Cut two 2⅞"-wide strips, then cut the strips into twenty 2⅞" squares. Cut each square in half diagonally to make 20 half-square triangles (C).

Cut one 3⅜"-wide strip, then cut the strip into eight 3⅜" squares. Cut each square in half diagonally to make 16 half-square triangles (H).

*Greens 2 and 3:* Cut one 3⅜"-wide strip of each color, then cut each strip into eight 3⅜" squares. Cut each square in half diagonally to make 16 half-square triangles (H).

### Bonnie Markham

As the proprietor of Grandma's Attic, Waterford's only quilt shop, Bonnie Markham provides local quilters with every sort of fabric, notion, pattern, or book they could wish for, but more importantly, she offers them a cozy, friendly gathering place and a sense of community. She enjoys folk music and cooking, interests which sometimes show up in the titles of her quilts. Her favorite patterns are traditional blocks such as Bear's Paw and Pinwheel, which she enjoys piecing from cottons in country colors or from homespuns. Her wardrobe includes many quilted vests and jackets, which she makes herself. She also enjoys Celtic knot-work appliqué, and usually creates her own patterns from designs she finds in books and jewelry.

### Craig Markham

Craig Markham is a proud Penn State graduate and Nittany Lions fan currently employed by the Office of the Physical Plant at Waterford College. In sharp contrast to his warm, empathetic wife, Bonnie, Craig has difficulty expressing—or even understanding—his own feelings. Thus, when he and Bonnie grow apart, he unwisely risks his marriage by engaging in a cyber affair instead of confronting his dissatisfaction honestly and openly. This same reserve leads him to express his remorse by cooking Bonnie dinner, since he cannot find the words to apologize.

*Blue 1:* Cut two 2½"-wide strips, then cut the strips into twenty 2½" squares (D).

Cut one 3⅜"-wide strip, then cut the strip into eight 3⅜" squares. Cut each square in half diagonally to make 16 half-square triangles (H).

*Blue 2:* Cut one 3⅜"-wide strip, then cut the strip into eight 3⅜" squares. Cut each square in half diagonally to make 16 half-square triangles (H).

*Red 1:* Cut one 3⅞"-wide strip, then cut the strip into ten 3⅞" squares. Cut each square in half diagonally to make 20 half-square triangles (E).

Cut one 3⅜"-wide strip, then cut the strip into eight 3⅜" squares. Cut each square in half diagonally to make 16 half-square triangles (H).

Cut four 3"-wide strips for the inner border.

*Red 2:* Cut one 3⅜"-wide strip, then cut the strip into eight 3⅜" squares. Cut each square in half diagonally to make 16 half-square triangles (H).

*Golds 1 and 2:* Cut one 3⅜"-wide strip of each color, then cut each strip into eight 3⅜" squares. Cut each square in half diagonally to make 16 half-square triangles (H).

## Double Heart Blossom Block Assembly

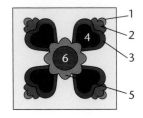

*Double Heart blossom Block*

The patterns are on page 50.

1. Refer to Quilting 101, page 93, for appliqué preparation and instructions. Use your favorite method to appliqué the shapes, following the numerical order on the diagram. Make 4 blocks.

2. Press and trim each block to 10½" square.

## Large Broken Dishes Block Assembly

1. Sew a background triangle (B) to a green triangle (C). Press seam toward green fabric. Make 40 B/C units.

*Make 40.*

2. Sew a red half-square triangle (E) to a tan half-square triangle (F). Press the seam toward the red fabric. Make 20 red and tan E/F units.

*Make 20.*

3. Sew 4 half-square triangle units (E/F) together as shown to make the center of each block.

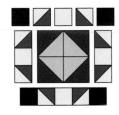

*Make 5.*

4. Sew the B/C and E/F units together with squares (A) and (D) into rows. Press. Make 5 blocks.

*Make 5.*

## Small Broken Dishes Border Blocks Assembly

1. Sew a background triangle (G) to a triangle (H) in Green 2 and 3, Blue 1 and 2, Red 1 and 2, and Gold 1 and 2. Press the seam toward the dark fabric. Make 16 G/H triangle units of each color combination (128 total).

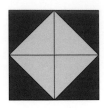

*Make 128 total.*

**2.** Sew 2 G/H units made using one color to 2 G/H units made using the second fabric in the same colorway to make 1 Broken Dish block. Make 8 blocks of each colorway for the Broken Dishes border (32 blocks total).

*Make 8 blocks of each colorway.*

## QUILT ASSEMBLY

**1.** Sew the pieced blocks and appliqué blocks into rows. Press the seams of alternating rows in opposite directions.

**2.** Sew the rows together and press.

## BORDERS

### Inner Borders

**1.** Refer to Quilting 101, page 93, for adding borders. Cut two 3" x 30½" strips for the sides and 3" x 35½" strips for the top and bottom inner borders. Sew to the sides and then top and bottom of the quilt top.

**2.** Press the seams toward the inner borders.

### Small Broken Dishes Border Assembly

*Note: Refer to the Quilt Assembly Diagram before sewing the border Broken Dishes blocks together. The blocks are sewn together in a different orientation for the side borders than they are for the top and bottom borders.*

**1.** Sew 7 small Broken Dishes blocks together to make each side border. Press. Sew to the sides of the quilt top. Press the seams toward the inner border.

**2.** Sew 9 small Broken Dishes blocks together to make each top and bottom border. Press. Sew the borders to the top and bottom of the quilt top. Press the seams toward the inner border.

### Outer Border

**1.** Sew the 1¼" strips end to end and cut two 1¼" x 45½" side outer borders and two 1¼" x 47" top and bottom borders. Sew the outer borders to the sides and then the top and bottom of the quilt. Press the seams toward the outer borders.

**2.** Refer to Quilting 101, page 94, to layer the quilt top, batting, and backing; baste. Quilt as desired. Bind.

*Quilt Assembly Diagram*

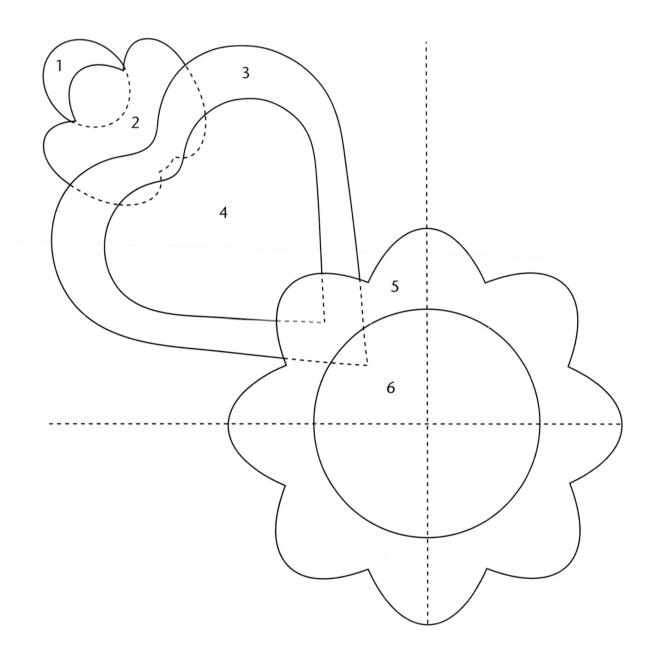

When He Makes Dinner
Double Heart Blossom

Quilting detail.

*When she opened the door, the delicious smells of cooking floated on the air, momentarily confusing her. Had she started dinner already and forgotten? She went to the kitchen, only to find Craig peering into the oven. The kitchen counter was littered with pans and Styrofoam meat trays and spice jars.*

*"What on earth?" Bonnie exclaimed, taking in the scene.*

*Craig jumped, startled, and shut the oven. "Hi, honey" he said, coming forward to kiss her on the cheek. "Dinner will be another fifteen minutes or so. I think. The recipe on the back of the soup can called it 'Easy Twenty-Minute Chicken,' but I think that's a typo. It's taken me forty minutes already." He shrugged and smiled. "Of course, I haven't done this in a while, so maybe it's me. The table's already set, so why don't you go change out of your work clothes and lie down for a while? I'll call you when it's ready."*

*Bonnie promptly burst into tears.*

Excerpted from *Round Robin*
by Jennifer Chiaverini

# The CROSS-COUNTRY QUILTERS

## Grace Daniels

A well-known quilt artist and historian, Grace Daniels also works as a curator for the De Young Museum in San Francisco. After a long dry spell in which she struggles to reconnect with her creativity, Grace comes to terms with a diagnosis of Multiple Sclerosis and resolves to continue quilting as long as possible. Taking inspiration from her good friend, Sylvia Compson, she resolves to find other artistic outlets if and when that path is closed to her.

## Megan Donohue

Megan attends Elm Creek Quilt Camp for the first time after winning a week's stay in a design contest for a quilting magazine. A fan of one-patch quilts and watercolor techniques, Megan lives with her nine-year-old son in Ohio, where she works as an aerospace engineer.

## Donna Jorgenson

A homemaker and mother of two, Donna confesses to being a compulsive fabric shopper with an embarrassing large accumulation of Unfinished Fabric Objects. Generous with her time and sensitive to the feelings of others, she is sometimes troubled by self-doubt, worrying that she has not set a good enough example for her daughters through her life choices. Her husband and many friends know better.

## Julia Merchaud

The winner of four Emmys and a Golden Globe, Julia Merchaud most recently starred as Grandma Wilson on the acclaimed primetime drama *Family Tree*. After the show is canceled, Julia expands her career into feature films. Although she has never sewn, she is offered a role in a historical movie when her agent passes her off as an accomplished quilter. With some misgivings, she attends Elm Creek Quilt Camp for a crash course.

For the quilt from *The Cross-Country Quilters*, I combined elements of the sampler quilt from *The Quilter's Apprentice* with the group quilt concept of *Round Robin*. In this novel, the five protagonists work on a unique "Challenge Quilt." After they become friends and share confidences at quilt camp, Vinnie, Grace, Megan, Donna, and Julia vow to overcome certain obstacles in their lives before they reunite a year later at Elm Creek Manor. As a reminder of their promise, they divide a piece of fabric into equal shares and agree to piece a block symbolic of their personal goals—but they may not begin their block until they have begun to resolve certain conflicts in their lives. In designing this quilt, as in the *Elm Creek Medallion*, I needed to choose blocks that appropriately symbolized the characters' struggles, but as in *Sarah's Sampler*, I wanted to choose blocks that harmonized with each other. I also chose blocks that suited the character's skills, which is why beginning quilter Julia pieces a simple Friendship Star, and Grace, an accomplished quilter and quilt historian, makes the more complex Carpenter's Wheel. I selected the Autumn Leaf blocks for the border to echo the autumn leaf print of the challenge fabric.

Machine pieced and hand quilted by Jennifer Chiaverini, 2001.

Finished Size: 56" x 56"
Block Size: 12" finished
Number of Blocks: 9 for the quilt center and 24 blocks for the border

# CROSS-COUNTRY
# CHALLENGE

## FABRIC REQUIREMENTS

**Light background:** 3½ yards (includes inner border)

**Challenge fabric:** ⅝ yard (includes binding)

**Dark green:** ¼ yard

**Light green:** ⅛ yard

**Purple:** ¼ yard

**Blue:** ⅛ yard

**Burgundy red:** ¼ yard

**Assorted medium and dark leaf fabrics:** 3 yards total

**Brown:** ¼ yard (appliquéd leaf stems)

**Backing:** 3⅜ yards

**Batting:** 60" x 60"

**Template plastic**

**Fusible paper-backed adhesive** (optional)

## BEAR'S PAW BLOCK

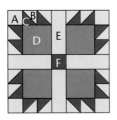

## Cutting

*Light background:* Cut four 2¼" squares (A).

Cut one 2⅝"-wide strip, then cut the strip into eight 2⅝" squares. Cut each square in half diagonally to make 16 half-square triangles (B).

Cut one 2"-wide strip, then cut the strip into four 2" x 5¾" rectangles (E).

*Purple:* Cut one 2⅝"-wide strip, then cut the strip into eight 2⅝" squares. Cut each square in half diagonally to make 16 half-square triangles (C).

Cut one 2" square (F).

*Challenge fabric:* Cut four 4" squares (D).

## Block Assembly

**1.** Sew triangles (B and C) together to make 16 B/C units.

*Make 16.*

**2.** Sew a square (A), 4 B/C units, and a square (D) together as shown. Make 4. Press.

*Make 4.*

**3.** Sew 4 Bear's Paw units, 4 background rectangles (E), and one center square (F) together to make a Bear Paw block. Press.

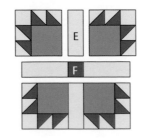

*Bear Paw Block Assembly*

## SNOW CRYSTALS BLOCK

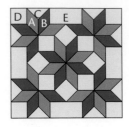

## Cutting

*Light background:* Cut two 3¾" squares, then cut each square into quarters twice diagonally into quarters to make 8 quarter-square triangles (C).

Cut two 2¼"-wide strips, then cut the strips into twelve 2¼" squares (D) and four 2¼" x 4" rectangles (E).

*Dark Green:* Using the Cross Country Diamond pattern, page 60, cut 16 diamonds (A).

*Challenge fabric:* Using the Cross Country Diamond pattern, page 60, cut 16 diamonds (B).

## Block Assembly

**1.** Refer to Quilting 101, page 91, for Y-seam construction. Make 8 A/B/C units. Backstitch at the dot. Press.

*Make 8.*

**2.** Sew one background square (D) to 2 A/B/C units using the Y-seam construction technique. Backstitch at the dot. Press. Make 4 A/B/C/D corner units.

*Make 4.*

**3.** Using Y-seam construction, make 4 A/B/D units. Backstitch at the dot. Press.

*Make 4.*

**4.** Sew 4 A/B/D units together as shown to make the center star. Backstitch at the dot. Press.

*Block Center Assembly*

**5.** Using Y-seam construction, sew 4 A/B/D units for the outside of the star's center. Backstitch at the dots. Press.

*Make 4.*

**6.** Using Y-seam construction, sew the 4 A/B/D units to the center star unit. Sew in the direction of the arrows, backstitch in the dots and at the star points. Press.

*Center Star Assembly*

**7.** Sew 4 background rectangles (E) and 4 corner units to the sides of the center star. Sew in the direction of the arrows, backstitching at the dots. Press.

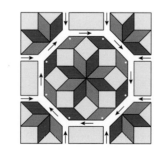

*Snow Crystals Block Assembly*

# FRIENDSHIP STAR BLOCK

## Cutting

*Light background:* Cut four 4 1/2" squares (A).

Cut two 4 7/8" squares, then cut each square in half diagonally to make 4 half-square triangles (B).

*Challenge fabric:* Cut two 4 7/8" squares, then cut each square in half diagonally to make 4 half-square triangles (C).

Cut one 4 1/2" square (D).

## Block Assembly

**1.** Make 4 half-square triangle B/C units. Press.

*Make 4.*

**2.** Sew squares (A and D) and B/C units together. Press.

*Friendship Star Block Assembly*

# CARPENTER'S WHEEL BLOCK

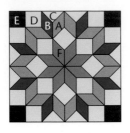

## Cutting

*Light background:* Cut two 3³/₄"
squares, then cut each square twice
diagonally into quarters to make 8
quarter-square triangles (C).

Cut one 2¹/₄"-wide strip, then cut the
strip into sixteen 2¹/₄" squares (D).

*Light green:* Using the Diamond pattern on page 60, cut 16 diamonds (A).

*Dark green:* Using the Diamond pattern on page 60, cut 8 diamonds (B).

*Burgundy red:* Cut four 2¹/₄" corner
squares (E).

*Challenge fabric:* Using the Diamond
pattern on page 60, cut 8 diamonds (F).

## Block Assembly

**1.** Refer to Quilting 101, page 91, for
Y-seam construction. Make 4 A/B/C
units and 4 mirror-image A/B/C
units. Backstitch at the dot. Press.

*Make 4.*

*Make 4.*

**2.** Using Y-Seam construction, make
4 A/A/D units. Sew in the direction
of the arrows, backstitching at the
dot. Press.

*Make 4.*

**3.** Sew squares E and D to the
A/A/D unit. Make 4. Press.

*Make 4.*

**4.** Sew 2 A/B/C units and 1 A/D/E
unit together to make 4 corner units.
Sew in the direction of the arrows,
backstitching at the dots. Press.

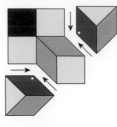

*Corner Unit*

**5.** Using Y-seam construction, make
4 F/F/D units. Sew in the direction
of the arrows, backstitching at the
dot. Press.

*Make 4.*

**6.** Sew 4 F/F/D units together to
make the center star of the block.
Sew in direction of the arrows, backstitching at the dots. Press.

*Block Center Assembly*

**7.** Sew the 4 corner units to the 4
sides of the center star. Sew in the
direction of the arrows, backstitching
at the dots and center star points.
Press.

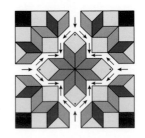

*Carpenter's Wheel Block Assembly*

## WEDDING RING BLOCK

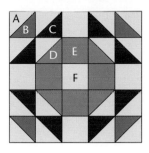

*Note: This 5-grid block does not fit easily into a 12" block, so the pieces are cut using 1/16" measurements. When cutting, place your fabric half way between the 1/8" marks on your ruler.*

## Cutting

**Light background:** Cut one 3⁵/₁₆"-wide strip (just slightly less than 3³/₈"). Cut the strip into eight 3⁵/₁₆" squares, then cut each square in half diagonally to make 16 half-square triangles (A).

Cut one 2¹⁵/₁₆"-wide strip, then cut the strip into five 2¹⁵/₁₆" squares (F).

**Blue:** Cut two 3⁵/₁₆" squares, then cut each square in half diagonally to make 4 half-square triangles (B).

**Burgundy red:** Cut four 3⁵/₁₆" squares, then cut each square in half diagonally to make 8 half-square triangles (C).

**Challenge fabric:** Cut two 3⁵/₁₆" squares, then cut each square in half diagonally to make 4 half-square triangles (D).

Cut four 2¹⁵/₁₆" squares (E).

## Block Assembly

**1.** Make 4 A/B half-square triangle units, 8 A/C half-square triangle units, and 4 A/D half-square triangle units. Press the seams toward the dark triangle.

*Make 4.*　　　*Make 8.*

*Make 4.*

**2.** Sew the blocks together into rows. Press.

**3.** Sew the rows together. Press.

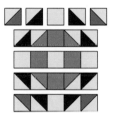

*Wedding Ring Block Assembly*

## LEAF BLOCKS BORDER

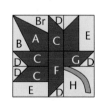

## Cutting

**Light background:** Using Cross Country Leaf B pattern on page 60, cut 24. Turn template over and cut 24 reversed.

*Note: If you cut the strips approximately 4⁷/₈"-wide and place the strips wrong sides together, you can cut the Leaf B pieces and the bottom strip will automatically be cut into the reversed Leaf B pieces.*

Cut thirteen 2"-wide strips, then cut the strips into 144–2" squares (D) and forty-eight 2" x 4" rectangles (E).

Cut three 3¹/₂"-wide strips, then cut the strips into twenty-four 3¹/₂" squares (H).

**Brown:** Using Cross Country Leaf Stem pattern, cut 24 stems.

**Assorted mediums and darks:** Using Cross Country Leaf A pattern, cut one for each leaf (24 total).

Cut four 2" x 4" rectangles (C) for each leaf (96 total).

Cut one 2" x 5" rectangle (F) for each leaf (24 total).

Cut one 2" x 3¹/₂" rectangle (G) for each leaf (24 total).

## Block Assembly

**1.** Sew 1 B, 1 B reversed, and 1 A together. Press.

*Leaf point*

**2.** Sew a square (D) to the right end of a rectangle (C) using a diagonal seam at the angle shown. Trim and press. Make 2 C/D units.

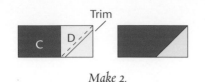

*Make 2.*

**3.** Sew a square (D) to the left end of a rectangle (C) using a diagonal seam at the angle shown. Trim and press. Make 2 reversed C/D units.

*Make 2.*

**4.** Sew a C/D unit and a reversed C/D unit together. Press. Make 2 units.

*Make 2.*

**5.** Sew a square (D) to the right end of a rectangle (F) using a diagonal seam at the angle shown. Trim and press.

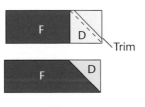

*Make 1.*

**6.** Sew a square (D) to the right end of a rectangle (G) using a diagonal seam at the angle shown. Trim and press.

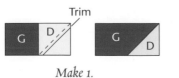

*Make 1.*

**7.** Appliqué the leaf stem onto background square (H) using your favorite method.

*Make 1.*

**8.** Sew the units together to make a leaf block. Press.

*Make 24 leaves total.*

## QUILT ASSEMBLY

*Light background:* Cut four 12½" squares.

**1.** Sew the pieced blocks and 12½" alternate blocks together into rows. Press toward the alternate blocks.

**2.** Sew the rows together. Press.

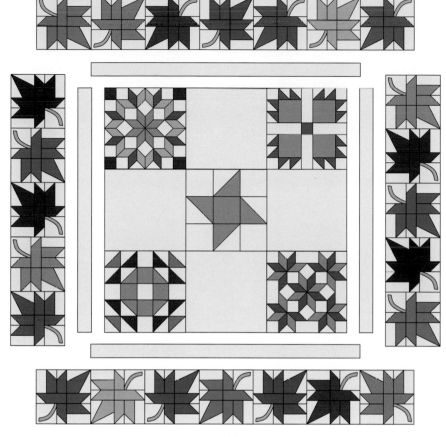

*Quilt Assembly Diagram*

## INNER BORDER

Refer to Quilting 101, page 93, for adding borders. For ease in piecing, we added a 2"-wide inner spacer border.

## Cutting

*Light background:* Cut four 2¹/₂"-wide strips.

## Assembly

**1.** Cut two 2¹/₂" x 36¹/₂" side inner borders and two 2¹/₂" x 40¹/₂" top and bottom borders. Sew the borders to the sides and then the top and bottom of the quilt top. Press the seams toward the border.

**2.** Sew 5 Leaf blocks together to make each side border. Note the rotation of the Leaf blocks above. Make 2. Press.

**3.** Sew 7 Leaf blocks together to make each top and bottom border. Note the rotation of the Leaf blocks above. Press. Sew the leaf borders to the sides and then the top and bottom of the quilt top. Press the seams toward the inner border.

**4.** Refer to Quilting 101, page 94, to layer the quilt top, batting, and backing; baste. Quilt as desired. Bind.

*T*he Cross-Country Quilters took turns telling onlookers the story of how their project had come to be, how each had faced a challenge in her life and had commemmorated her success, but by unspoken agreement, the Cross-Country Quilters refused to divulge the confidences of their friends. Grace had the final word that put an end to the persistent inquiries: "Think of the challenges you face as a woman, as a wife, as a mother. The problems we faced were no different than those any woman faces."

Excerpted from *The Cross-Country Quilters* by Jennifer Chiaverini

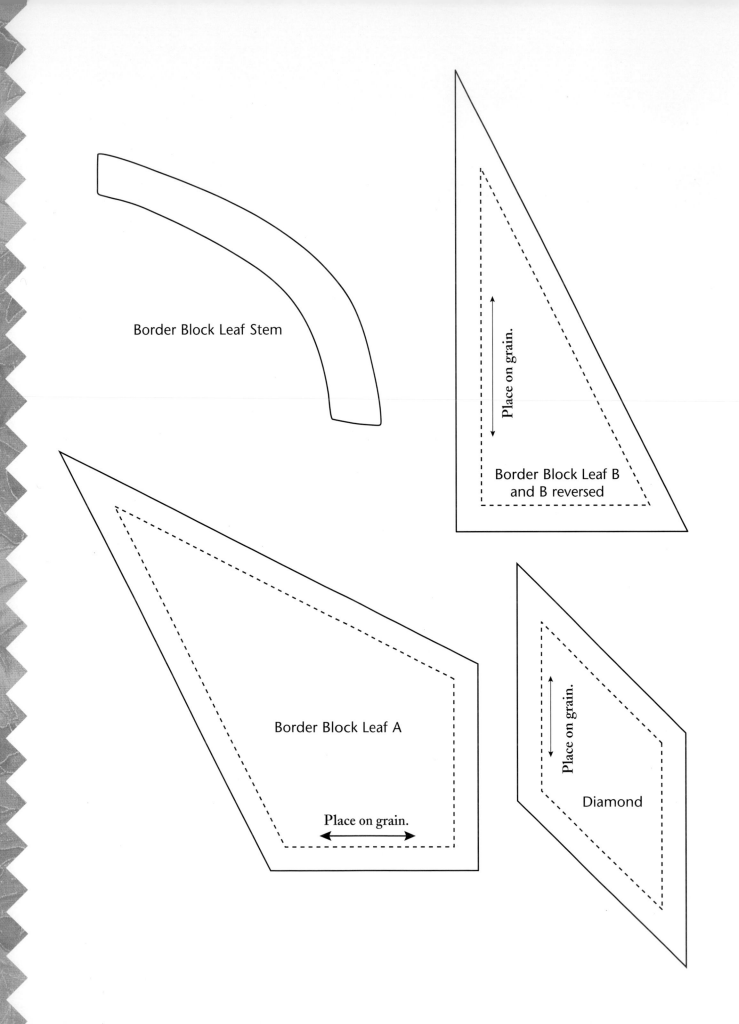

Border Block Leaf Stem

Border Block Leaf B
and B reversed

Place on grain.

Border Block Leaf A

Place on grain.

Diamond

Place on grain.

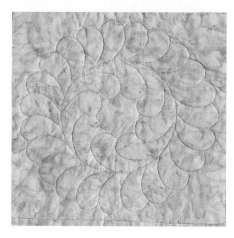

Quilting design for alternate blocks

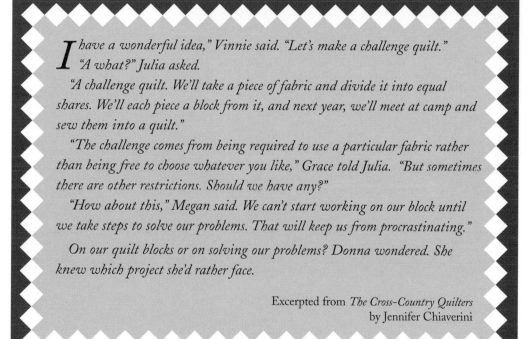

*I* have a wonderful idea," Vinnie said. "Let's make a challenge quilt."

"A what?" Julia asked.

"A challenge quilt. We'll take a piece of fabric and divide it into equal shares. We'll each piece a block from it, and next year, we'll meet at camp and sew them into a quilt."

"The challenge comes from being required to use a particular fabric rather than being free to choose whatever you like," Grace told Julia. "But sometimes there are other restrictions. Should we have any?"

"How about this," Megan said. We can't start working on our block until we take steps to solve our problems. That will keep us from procrastinating."

On our quilt blocks or on solving our problems? Donna wondered. She knew which project she'd rather face.

Excerpted from *The Cross-Country Quilters*
by Jennifer Chiaverini

Machine pieced by Nancy Odom and quilted by Linda Leathersich, 2002.

*Fabrics for this project were graciously donated by P&B Textiles.*

Finished Size: 86" x 109"
Block Size: 18" finished
Number of Blocks: 12 with 20 small Pinwheel blocks in the sashing

# Vinnie's Double Pinwheel

## FABRIC REQUIREMENTS

**Blue:** 7/8 yard

**Orange:** 7/8 yard

**Yellow:** 7/8 yard

**Green:** 7/8 yard

**Red:** 3 3/8 yards

**Black:** 5 1/4 yards (includes binding)

**Backing:** 7 5/8 yards

**Batting:** 90" x 113"

## Cutting

Patterns are on page 67.

*Blue:* Cut one 6⅞"-wide strip, then cut each strip into six 6⅞" squares. Cut each square in half diagonally to make 12 half-square triangles (A).

Cut one 3⅞"-wide strip, then cut each strip into six 3⅞" squares. Cut each square in half diagonally to make 12 half-square triangles (C).

Cut one 10¼"-wide strip, then cut each strip into three 10¼" squares. Cut each square twice diagonally into quarters to make 12 quarter-square triangles (G).

*Orange:* Cut one 6⅞"-wide strip, then cut each strip into six 6⅞" squares. Cut each square in half diagonally to make 12 half-square triangles (A).

Cut one 3⅞"-wide strip, then cut each strip into six 3⅞" squares. Cut each square in half diagonally to make 12 half-square triangles (C).

Cut one 10¼"-wide strip, then cut each strip into three 10¼" squares. Cut each square twice diagonally into quarters to make 12 quarter-square triangles (G).

*Yellow:* Cut one 6⅞"-wide strip, then cut each strip into six 6⅞" squares. Cut each square in half diagonally to make 12 half-square triangles (A).

Cut one 3⅞"-wide strip, then cut each strip into six 3⅞" squares. Cut each square in half diagonally to make 12 half-square triangles (C).

Cut one 10¼"-wide strip, then cut each strip into three 10¼" squares. Cut each square twice diagonally into quarters to make 12 quarter-square triangles (G).

*Green:* Cut one 6⅞"-wide strip, then cut each strip into six 6⅞" squares. Cut each square in half diagonally to make 12 half-square triangles (A).

Cut one 3⅞"-wide strip, then cut each strip into six 3⅞" squares. Cut each square in half diagonally to make 12 half-square triangles (C).

Cut one 10¼"-wide strip, then cut each strip into three 10¼" squares. Cut each square twice diagonally into quarters to make 12 quarter-square triangles (G).

*Red:* Using Vinnie's Double Pinwheel pattern E, cut 48 trapezoids (E).

Cut four 3⅜"-wide strips, then cut the strips into forty 3⅜" squares. Cut each square in half diagonally to make 80 triangles for the sashing Pinwheels.

*Lavina Burkholder (Vinnie)*

Octogenarian Vinnie Burkholder—or Nana, as she likes anyone under thirty to call her—was one of the first quilters to attend Elm Creek Quilt Camp. A longtime resident of Dayton, Ohio, Vinnie is a member of a quilt guild that meets in her retirement community; her favorite part of the meetings is the show and tell. She often selects a new project based upon the block name rather than its appearance, and currently has a particular affinity for the Wedding Ring, Double Wedding Ring, and Steps to the Altar patterns. Vinnie prefers bright colors, which reflect her sunny outlook on life, and she is always eager to learn a new quilting technique or try out a new gadget.

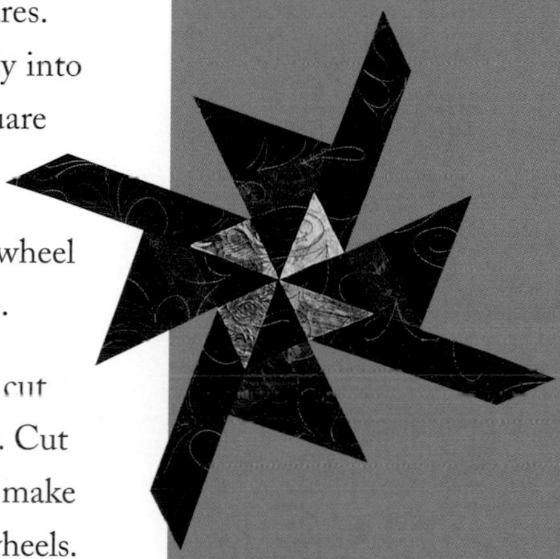

Cut sixteen 5½"-wide strips, then cut the strips into thirty-one 5½" x 18½" rectangles for sashing strips.

*Black:* Using Vinnie's Double Pinwheel pattern B, cut 48 parallelograms.

Cut three 3⅞"-wide strips, the cut the strips into 24 squares. Cut each square in half diagonally to make 48 black triangles (F).

Cut four 5⅜"-wide strips, then cut the strips into twenty-four squares. Cut the squares in half diagonally to make 48 black triangles for pinwheels (D).

Cut four 3⅜"-wide strips, then cut the strips into forty squares. Cut each square in half diagonally to make 80 triangles for the sashing pinwheels.

Cut eleven 6½"-wide strips for the border.

## DOUBLE PINWHEEL BLOCK

*Make 12 of each color: blue, green, yellow, and orange.*

## Block Assembly

**1.** Sew triangle (A) to black trapezoid (B). Press. Then sew the A/B unit to triangle (C). Press. Make 12 A/B/C units of each color blue, green, yellow, orange.

*Make 12 of each color.*

**2.** Sew black triangle (D) to red piece (E). Then sew the D/E unit to black triangle (F). Press. Make 48 D/E/F units.

**3.** Sew a D/E/F unit to a quarter-square triangle (G). Press. Make 12 units of each color: blue, green, yellow, orange.

*Make 12 of each color.*

**4.** Sew the 2 units together to make one quarter of the block. Press. Repeat to make 12 of each color. Refer to the quilt photo for color placement.

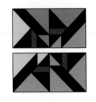

*Make 12 of each color.*

**5.** Sew the 4 quarters of the block together to complete the block. Press.

*Double Pinwheel Block Assembly*

## Pinwheel Sashing Blocks

Sew together black and red triangles to make 40 half-square triangle units. Press the seam toward the black triangle.

*Make 80.*

**2.** Sew the units together to make 20 pinwheels. Press.

*Make 20.*

## QUILT ASSEMBLY

**1.** Refer to the Assembly Diagram and quilt photo to lay out blocks and sashing.

**2.** Sew the Double Pinwheel blocks, sashing Pinwheel blocks, and sashing strips into rows. Press the seams toward the sashing.

**3.** Sew the block rows and sashing rows together. Press the seams toward the sashing rows.

**4.** Refer to Quilting 101, page 93, for adding borders. Sew the 6½"-wide border strips end to end and cut two 6½" x 97½" side borders, and two 6½" x 86½" top and bottom borders.

**5.** Sew the borders to the sides and then the top and bottom of the quilt top. Press the seams toward the border.

**6.** Refer to Quilting 101, page 94, to layer the quilt top, batting, and backing; baste. Quilt as desired. Bind.

*Quilt Assembly Diagram*

*Vinnie showed off a half-finished Double Pinwheel quilt top she had worked on in her Quick Piecing classes, and declared that her favorite memory was her surprise birthday party. "That's what you said last year," Sylvia said, her eyes glinting with merriment, "and the year before. It's time for you to come up with something new."*

*Vinnie pursed her lips and thought, then said that if Sylvia wouldn't let her use her real favorite memory, she would have to go with the food.*

Excerpted from *The Cross-Country Quilters*
by Jennifer Chiaverini

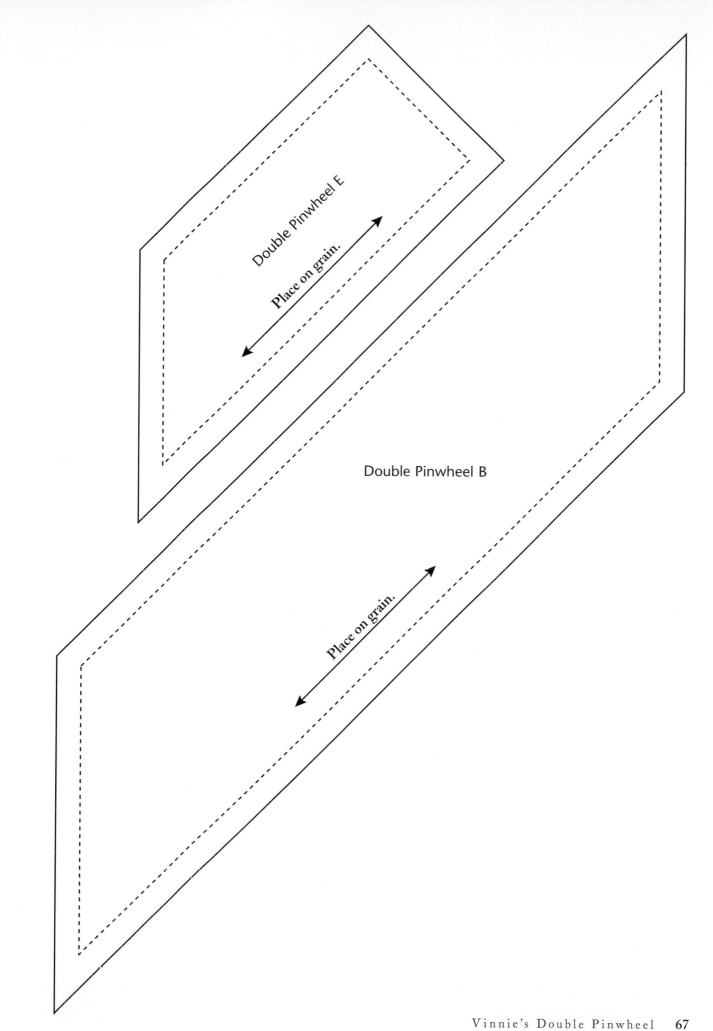

Double Pinwheel E

Place on grain.

Double Pinwheel B

Place on grain.

## The RUNAWAY QUILT

### Hans Bergstrom

Confident and independent, Hans prefers to make his own way in the world, but he is not above taking advantage of fools if he believes they deserve their misfortune. Though Hans takes ownership of Elm Creek Farm through somewhat questionable means, there is nothing to doubt in his steadfast hard work to establish himself in America or in his devotion to his wife, Anneke. An isolationist at heart, Hans prefers to mind his own business and leave the fight for the abolition of slavery to his sister, Gerda.

### Anneke Bergstrom

The youngest of the founders of Elm Creek Farm, Anneke marries Hans after her fiancé fails to meet her upon her arrival in America. Gerda is torn between pleasing her husband, who expects her to fulfill the traditional duties of wife and mother, and pursuing her own dream of running a thriving seamstress's shop. While her devotion to her family is one of her greatest strengths, it also makes her susceptible to deceit when unscrupulous enemies play on her fears for her family's safety.

### Joanna

Little is known of the runaway slave who affected the Bergstroms' lives so profoundly. She was likely born around 1830 in Wentworth County, Virginia, on a plantation owned by Josiah Chester. The very fact that she was able to endure the hardships of slavery and the hazards of her journey north prove that she was a woman of great fortitude, determination, and courage. Though she was recaptured before she could reach safety in Canada and was sold off to a plantation in South Carolina, her son was raised in freedom as a member of the Bergstrom family. Even after the war, the Bergstroms never learned Joanna's fate.

Like many quilters, I have been fascinated by the stories of signal quilts used along the Underground Railroad. The folklore so captivated my imagination that I included the legend of the Log Cabin block with a black center square in my first novel, *The Quilter's Apprentice*, in which Sylvia mentions that her great-grandparents had sheltered runaway slaves on their Pennsylvania farm. Since the role of quilts on the Underground Railroad is inconclusive, as *The Runaway Quilt* unfolds, I try to provide an explanation for the evolution of the legends, honoring the oral tradition while also adhering to confirmed historical fact. In order to capture the essence of the era, I used Civil War reproduction fabrics in making the four quilts that figure prominently in this story of family secrets and the Underground Railroad. The first is *The Runaway Quilt* of the title, a Birds in the Air quilt Sylvia discovers in South Carolina that seems to have a mysterious connection to Elm Creek Manor. The second is a four-patch strip quilt called *Underground Railroad*, which, in the novel, sends a secret message to fugitive slaves that they will find sanctuary within the home. The third is a crib-sized *Birds in the Air* quilt, which the Bergstroms use as their signal quilt when their original signal is compromised. The fourth is a Log Cabin quilt, whose role in the Underground Railroad is perhaps the most hotly debated of all. I am grateful to my many readers who helped me complete my version of this beautiful quilt. The final quilt, *Joanna's Pumpkins and Pomegranates*, was inspired by the cover design by Honi Werner.

Machine pieced by Jennifer Chiaverini, machine quilted by Cathy Franks, 2002.

Finished Size: 59" x 76"
Block Size: 6" finished
Number of Blocks: 83

# The Runaway Quilt

## FABRIC REQUIREMENTS

**Light Background to total:** 2 1/2 yards

**Medium and dark scraps to total:** 3 yards

**Border:** 1 5/8 yards (includes binding)

**Backing:** 3 5/8 yards

**Batting:** 63" x 80"

## Cutting

*Birds in the Air block*

*Light background:* Cut twenty 2 7/8"-wide strips, then cut the strips into 249–2 7/8" squares. Cut each square in half diagonally to make 498 half-square triangles (A).

Cut two 9 3/4"-wide strips, then cut the strips into six 9 3/4" squares. Cut each square twice diagonally to make 24 large quarter-square setting triangles.

Cut two 5 1/8" squares, then cut each square in half diagonally to make 4 corner triangles.

*Medium and dark scraps:* Cut 125–2 7/8" squares, then cut each square in half diagonally to make 249 half-square triangles (B).

Cut forty-two 6 7/8" squares, then cut each square in half diagonally to make 84 half-square triangles (C).

*Dark:* Cut eight 4 1/2"-wide strips for the border.

## Block Assembly

**1.** Sew a background triangle (A) to a medium or dark triangle (B). Press the seam toward the darker fabric. Make 3 for each block (249 total).

*Make 3 for each block.*

**2.** Sew 3 A/B units and three background triangles (A) into 3 rows. Press the seams for each row in opposite directions. Sew the rows together. Press.

*Partial Block Assembly*

**3.** Sew a large triangle (C) to a pieced A/B triangle unit. Press the seam toward the large triangle. Make 83 blocks.

*Make 83 blocks.*

## QUILT ASSEMBLY

**1.** Sew the pieced blocks and the setting triangles into diagonal rows. Press the seams of each row in opposite directions.

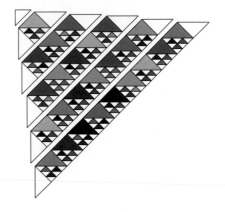

*Quilt Assembly Diagram for diagonal rows*

**2.** Sew the diagonal rows together. Add the 4 corner triangles to finish the top. Press.

**3.** Refer to Quilting 101, page 93, for adding borders. Sew border strips end to end and trim to make two 4 1/2" x 68 1/2" side borders and two 4 1/2" x 59 1/2" top and bottom borders. Sew to the sides and then the top and bottom of the quilt top. Press the seams towards the border.

**4.** Refer to Quilting 101, page 94, to layer the quilt top, batting, and backing; baste. Quilt as desired. Bind.

*Quilt Assembly Diagram*

*S*he [Sylvia] had heard of such things before, quilts with coded messages or
even maps revealing safe pathways along the Underground Railroad. The
very name of Margaret's quilt suggested it might be one of those legendary
artifacts. But in all of Sylvia's decades as a quilter and lecturer, she had never
seen one of these quilts, only heard lore of them around the quilt frame. Her
friend Grace Daniels, a master quilter and museum curator, had once told her
that not only had no one ever documented a map quilt from the era, no slave
narrator or Abolitionist testimonial she read mentioned one.

Excerpted from *The Runaway Quilt*
by Jennifer Chiaverini

Machine pieced by Nancy Odom and quilted by Linda Leathersich, 2002.
*Fabrics for this project were generously donated by Michael Miller Fabrics.*

Finished Size: 42" x 54"
Block Size: 6" finished
Number of Blocks: 48

# BIRDS IN THE AIR

## FABRIC REQUIREMENTS

**Background:** 1 yard

**Light:** ¾ yard

**Medium:** ¾ yard

**Dark:** 1⅜ yards (includes borders)

**Backing:** 1¾ yards

**Batting:** 46" x 58"

**Binding:** ½ yard

## Cutting

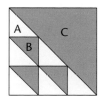

*Birds in the Air Block*

*Background:* Cut eleven 2⅞"-wide strips, then cut the strips into 144–2⅞" squares. Cut each square in half diagonally to make 288 half-square triangles (A).

*Lights:* Cut two 6⅞"-wide strips, then cut the strips into eight 6⅞" squares. Cut each square in half diagonally to make 16 half-square triangles (C).

Cut two 2⅞"-wide strips, then cut the strips into twenty-four 2⅞" squares. Cut each square in half diagonally to make 48 half-square triangles (B).

*Mediums:* Cut two 6⅞"-wide strips, then cut the strips into eight 6⅞" squares. Cut each square in half diagonally to make 16 half-square triangles (C).

Cut two 2⅞"-wide strips, then cut the strips into twenty-four 2⅞" squares. Cut each square in half diagonally to make forty-eight half-square triangles (B).

*Darks:* Cut two 6⅞"-wide strips, then cut the strips into eight 6⅞" squares. Cut each square in half diagonally to make 16 half-square triangles (C).

Cut two 2⅞"-wide strips, then cut the strips into twenty-four 2⅞" squares. Cut each square in half diagonally to make 48 half-square triangles (B).

Cut five 3½"-wide strips for the borders.

## Block Assembly

**1.** Follow Steps 1–3 of the Runaway Quilt Block Assembly instructions, page 70. Make 48 blocks total (16 with light, 16 with medium, and 16 with dark triangles).

*Make 16.*

*Make 16.*

*Make 16.*

## QUILT ASSEMBLY

**1.** Sew alternating light, medium, and dark blocks together into horizontal rows. Press the seams in alternate directions.

**2.** Sew the rows together. Press.

## BORDERS

**1.** Refer to Quilting 101, page 93, for adding borders. Sew the 3½"-wide border strips end to end and cut two 3½" x 48½" side borders and two 3½" x 42½" top and bottom borders. Sew the borders to the sides and then the top and bottom of the quilt top. Press the seams toward the border.

**2.** Refer to Quilting 101, page 94, to layer the quilt top, batting, and backing; baste. Quilt as desired. Bind.

*Quilt Assembly Diagram*

*Anneke declared she knew exactly the thing: a quilt pattern common enough that it would not attract unwanted attention, and yet simple enough that even I could fashion it well. It was called Birds in the Air, and as it was fashioned of many triangles, we could, by placement of the quilt upon the line, indicate in which direction the fugitives could find a safe haven.*

Excerpted from *The Runaway Quilt*
by Jennifer Chiaverini

*Quilting Detail.*

Each block for the front and back of this quilt was made by Jennifer's friends from throughout the United States and around the world. See page 79 for a complete list of the contributors. The quilt top and back were pieced by Jennifer, and machine quilted by Cathy Franks, 2002. Many thanks to all who helped make this wonderful quilt possible!

Finished Size: 70" x 98"
Block Size: 7" finished
Number of Blocks: 140 Log Cabin blocks in the Barn-Raising setting

# GERDA'S LOG CABIN

## FABRIC REQUIREMENTS

**Assorted lights to total:** 5½ yards

**Assorted darks to total:** 7 yards

**Black:** ½ yards

**Backing:** 5 ¾ yards

**Batting:** 74" x 102"

**Binding:** ¾ yard

## Cutting

*Note: The sizes of the strips listed are cut large so they can be trimmed after sewing.*

**Black:** Cut seven 2"-wide strips, then cut the strips into 140–2" squares (A).

**Light and Dark Fabrics:** Cut all light and dark fabrics into 2"-wide strips. You can precut the strip lengths, mixing up the fabrics in the light and dark areas, or you can pick strips at random and cut the lengths as you go.

## BLOCK ASSEMBLY

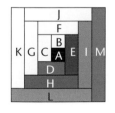

*Log Cabin Block*

Refer to Quilting 101, page 92, for the paper-piecing instructions to make Log Cabin blocks. Make 140 copies of the Log Cabin paper-piecing pattern, page 78, and paper piece the Log Cabin blocks. Make 140.

## QUILT ASSEMBLY

**1.** Sew the blocks together into horizontal rows. Remove the paper from the back of the blocks and press the seams of alternate rows in opposite directions.

**2.** Sew the horizontal rows together. Press the seams in one direction.

**3.** Refer to Quilting 101, page 94, to layer the quilt top, batting, and backing; baste. Quilt as desired. Bind.

*Quilt Assembly Diagram*

Gerda Bergstrom

Born in Baden-Baden, Germany, Gerda Bergstrom immigrates to the United States in 1856 to escape a broken heart and to join her brother, Hans, in his quest to make his fortune. Unlike her sister-in-law, Gerda despises sewing and learns to quilt only so that she might participate in the stimulating political discussions that take place at the home of the leader of the quilting circle. She gladly leaves the household sewing to her sister-in-law, and in her lifetime, makes only four quilts: a Shoo-Fly quilt for her bed, which due to her disinterest has a humility block in a very conspicuous place; a crib-size Birds in the Air quilt, which is actually a signal to fugitive slaves that Elm Creek Manor is a station on the Underground Railroad; a Churn Dash quilt; and a Log Cabin quilt made in remembrance of Joanna, a runaway slave who found sanctuary within Elm Creek Manor and became Gerda's friend before her recapture.

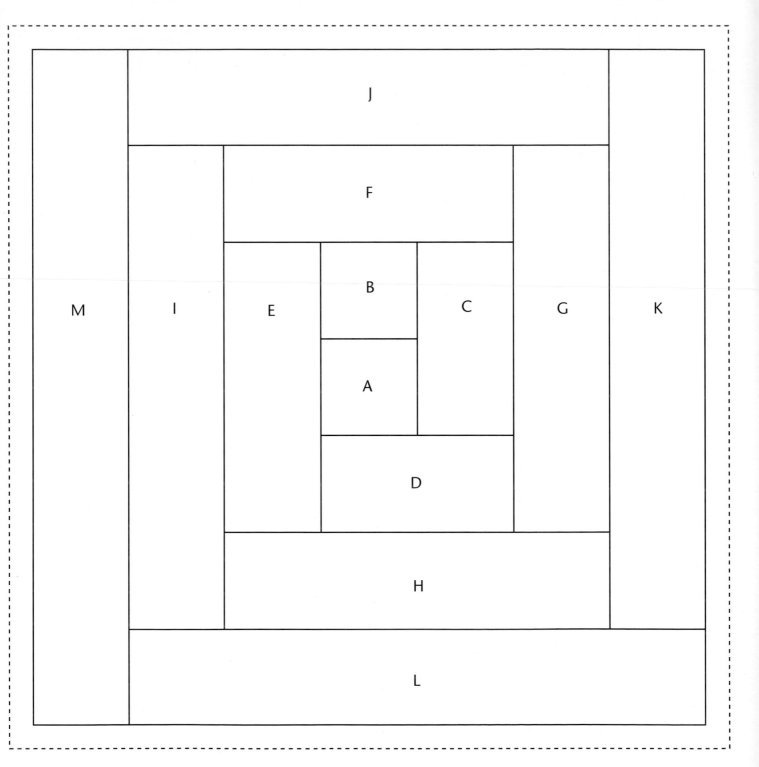

Gerda's Log Cabin Paper-Piecing Pattern

*Gerda's Log Cabin was made with the help of the following block contributors from across the United States and around the world.*
*Thanks to all of you special people!*

Geneva Adams
Mary Althaus
Phyllis Andersen
Vicki Anderson
Lynnis Baker
Johanna Balkany
Marjorie Bauer (La Cour)
Diane Beaudoin
Judy Beavers
Elaine Bednarz
Beverly Beyer
Kris Bishop
Cheryl Brinker
Christina Brode
Tracey K. Brown
Beth A. Burke
Linda Campbell
Carol Getz Candlish
Normand P. Caron
Pat Caron
Suellen Carroll
Janet Carruthers

Cathy Caviness
Jennifer Chiaverini
Bonnie L. Cirisan
Kimberly Clarke
Nadine Marx Cordio
Candy Couture
Annice Peckham Crandall
Jo Ann Creiglow
Jeanne W. Curran
Mary E. Curran
Sarah Curry
Virginia Davis
Corky Deibel
Sharon L. Eitniear
Trisha Eitniear
Roberta J. Estes
Katherine Fenn
Elizabeth Fletcher
Mary E. Fox
Susan Goecker
Nancy Goudy
Sally M. Graff
Ruth Reedy Green
Jacquelyn Greuel
Claire Halligan
Tutu Haynes-Smart
Judith Hechel

Alice M. Hesse
Kathy Hockings
Carolyn Holbrook
Connie Huhn-Melone
Barbara A. Johnson
Dianne Judd
Stephanie Kearns
Jennifer R. Keller
Suzanne Kelly
Jane Kenney
Susan Kirchner
Susie Klostermann (susie sews 4 u)
Georgette Kozloff
Judith Stapleman Kroes
Norma Kruger
Jean Landgraf
Dianne L. Larson
Linda Lazic
Betty A. Leduc
Kathleen A. Lee
Cathy Leitner
Sandie Lewis
Diane L. Leibenthal
Nancy Linnerooth
Beverly Macbeth
Monica A. MacDonald
Virginia Mallison

Sandra Marsh
Audrey Cripps McCormick
Judith T. Meyer
Amy S. Miga
Renee Miller
Patricia Mitchell
Alice L. Mott
Trish Myrick
Arlene Neale
Geraldine C. Neidenbach
Heather Neidenbach
Clare Nordman
Carol O'Connor
Clare K. O'Neil
Jackie O'Neill
Marilyn A. Palmer
Sharon Rose Pasma
Edna J. Porter
Jo-Ann Pouliot
Julie Powers
Sharon Raimondo
Laurie Reilly
Moira Riddell
Renee Rose
Carolyn Santoro
Dorothy L. Sauerwein
Sharyn Schnepel
Nancy Schrader
Judith Schustedt
Kay Schustedt
Pamela Schuster
Mary Schwantes
Judith Scowden
Elaine Scully
Mary Shaffer
Ruth Shaffer
Steven A. Sharp
Sue Shikany
Marilyn E. Sholtis
Kathy Silvon
Cathy Skelton (and Chester the Cat)
Peg Smith
Peggy Sperry
Peggy Spin
Faith Sullivan
Susan Sullivan
Mickie Swall
Annette Tallard
Jill M. Tasker
Mary Jean Thalaker
Mari-Jane Thurlow
Cheryl A. Tobin
Mary A. Umbeck
Carol A. Valenta
Greta VanDenBerg-Nestle
Barbara E. VanFossen
Yvonne Vesel
E. Rain Vincent
Sue Vollbrecht
Karen Waggoner
Judith H. Ward
Karen Sue Whiteside
Cindy Wilson
Margaret Winger
Connie Wood
Susan Woodward
Linda Workman
Alice Wurpel
Suzanne E. Zobel

Machine appliquéd and quilted by Nancy Odom, 2002.
*Fabrics for this project were generously donated by Benartex Fabrics.*

Finished Size: 57½" x 57½"
Center Block Size: 23½" x 23½" finished

# JOANNA'S PUMPKINS & POMEGRANATES

## FABRIC REQUIREMENTS

**Light background:** $2^{7}/_{8}$ yards

**Red:** $^{3}/_{4}$ yard

**Gold:** $^{3}/_{4}$ yard

**Green 1:** $1^{1}/_{8}$ yards

**Green 2:** $^{1}/_{3}$ yard

**Orange 1:** $^{3}/_{4}$ yard

**Orange 2:** $^{1}/_{3}$ yard

**Backing:** $3^{1}/_{2}$ yards

**Batting:** 62" x 62"

**Binding:** $^{1}/_{2}$ yard

$^{1}/_{4}$" **Bias bars for the vines** (optional)

**Template plastic** (optional)

**3 yards of fusible paper-backed adhesive** (optional)

## Cutting

Patterns are on pages 84–86.

*Light background:* Cut one 26" square for the center block.

Cut four 12" squares for the border corners.

Cut four 12"-wide strips for appliquéd borders.

*Red:* Cut four 2"-wide strips for the checkerboard border.

*Gold:* Cut four 2"-wide strips for the checkerboard border.

*Green 1:* Vines and Stems: Cut one 19" square, then cut $^{7}/_{8}$"-wide bias strips to total 350".

*Green 2:* Cut four $1^{1}/_{2}$"-wide strips for inner borders.

*Orange 1:* Cut six $3^{1}/_{2}$"-wide strips for the outer borders.

## CENTER APPLIQUÉ BLOCK AND APPLIQUÉ BORDER ASSEMBLY

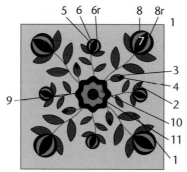

*Center Block Assembly Diagram*

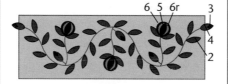

*Border Appliqué Diagram*

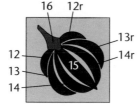

*Appliqué Border Corner*

**1.** Refer to Quilting 101, page 93, for preparation for appliqué. Lightly mark the placement of the appliqué shapes on the background center block, border strips, and border corner squares.

**2.** Use the patterns to prepare the appliqué pieces.

Cut the $^{7}/_{8}$"-wide bias strips to the lengths needed for the stems and vines. Each border vine will need a strip approximately 60" long. Sew strips end to end using a diagonal seam.

Use red to make 4 large pomegranates (7), 16 small pomegranates (5), 24 buds (3), and 1 center bloom (9).

Use gold to make 4 each large pomegranates details (8, 8R), 16 each small pomegranate details (6, 6R), and 1 center bloom (10).

Use green 2 to make 4 pumpkin stems (16).

Use green 1 to make approximately 350" of $^{7}/_{8}$"-wide bias strips, 24 buds (4), 16 large leaves (1), and 144 small leaves (2).

Use orange 1 to make 1 center bloom (11).

Use orange 2 to make 4 pumpkins (12, 12R, 13, 13R, 14, 14R, 15).

**3.** With wrong sides together, fold the bias strips in half lengthwise and sew about $^{1}/_{8}$" from the outside edge. Insert a bias bar, and press with the seam centered on the back.

**4.** Cut to the lengths needed and baste or lightly glue the vine sections onto the right side of the background fabric with the seam allowances facing down. Appliqué using your favorite method.

**5.** Appliqué the remaining shapes following the numerical order on the diagram. Reserve the buds that overlap the seams between the borders and the border corners. These buds will be added after the borders and corner blocks have been sewn to the quilt top.

**6.** Press. Trim the center block to 24" square, the borders to 10½" x 32", and the border corners to 10½" square.

## BORDERS

### Inner Border

**1.** Refer to Quilting 101, page 93, for adding borders. From the 1½"-wide strips, cut two 1½" x 24" side borders and two 1½" x 26" top and bottom borders.

**2.** Sew the borders to the sides and then to the top and bottom of the center square. Press the seams toward the border.

## Checkerboard Border

**1.** Sew a red and gold strip together along the long edge. Make 4 strip sets. Press the seam toward the red strip.

**2.** Cut the strip sets into seventy-six 2" units.

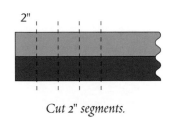

*Cut 2" segments.*

**3.** Rotate every other unit to create the checkerboard design. Sew 17 red/gold units together for each side border and 21 red/gold units for each top and bottom border. Press seams in one direction. Sew the side and then the top and bottom borders to the quilt top. Press the seams toward the inner border.

*Border Assembly*

## Appliqué Border

**1.** Sew the appliqué borders to the sides of the quilt top. Press seams toward appliqué borders.

**2.** Sew the appliqué corner blocks to each end of the two remaining appliqué borders. Refer to the Assembly Diagram for placement of the pumpkins. Press the seams away from the corner.

**3.** Sew the borders to the top and bottom of the quilt top. Press seams toward the appliqué borders.

**4.** Appliqué the final 8 buds over the corner seams.

## Outer Border

**1.** Refer to Quilting 101, page 93, for adding borders. Sew the 3½"-wide strips end to end to make two 3½" x 52" side borders and two 3½" x 58" top and bottom borders. Sew the side borders and then the top and bottom borders to the quilt top. Press the seams toward the border.

**2.** Refer to Quilting 101, page 94, to layer the quilt top, batting, and backing; baste. Quilt as desired. Bind.

*Quilt Assembly Diagram*

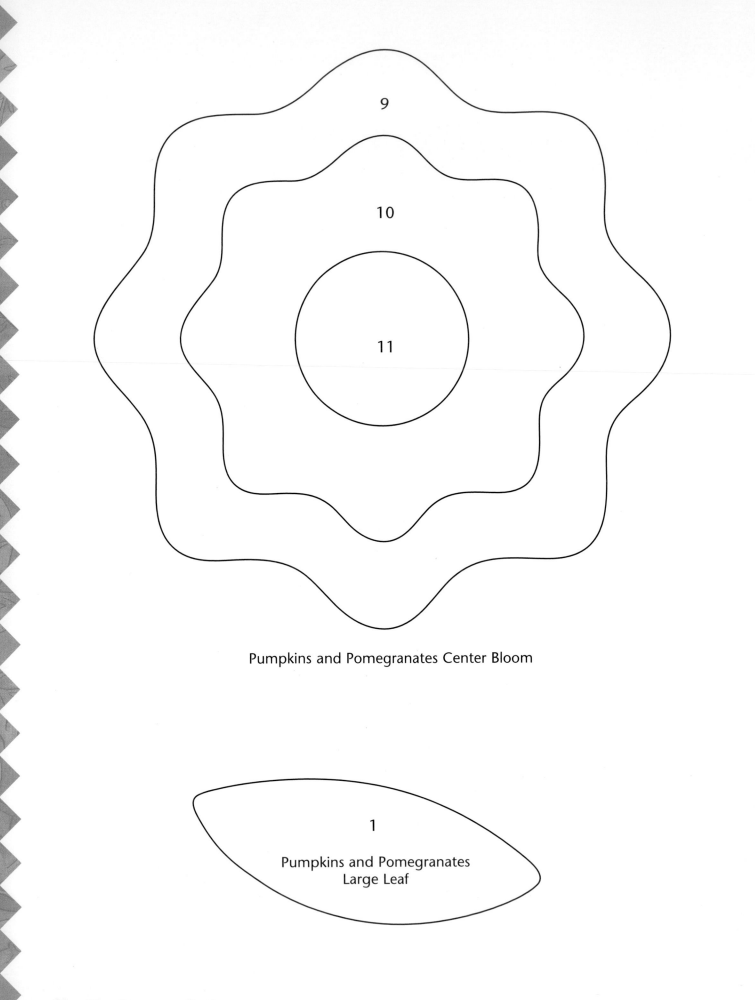

Pumpkins and Pomegranates Center Bloom

Pumpkins and Pomegranates
Large Leaf

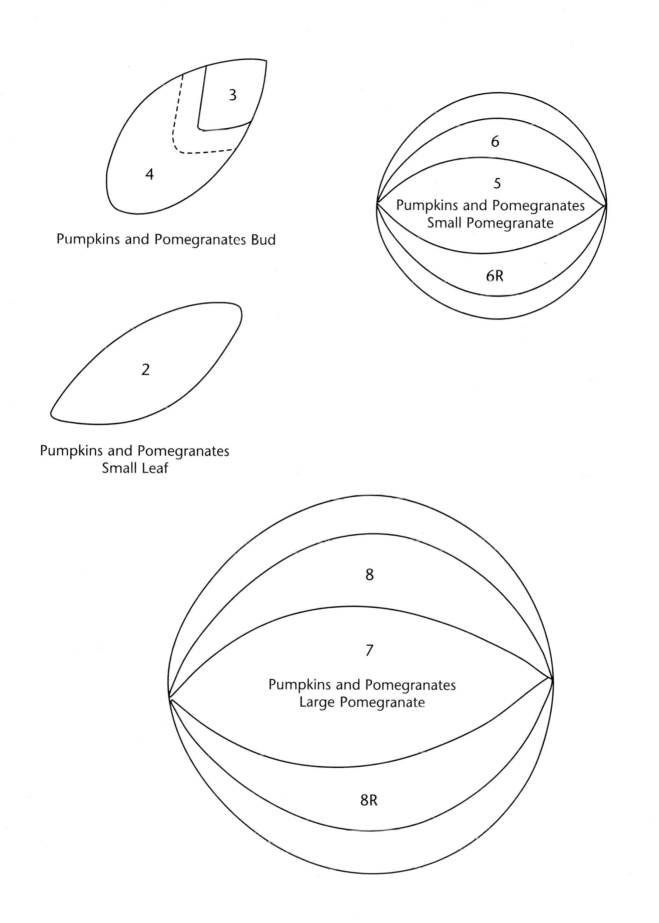

Pumpkins and Pomegranates Bud

Pumpkins and Pomegranates
Small Pomegranate

Pumpkins and Pomegranates
Small Leaf

Pumpkins and Pomegranates
Large Pomegranate

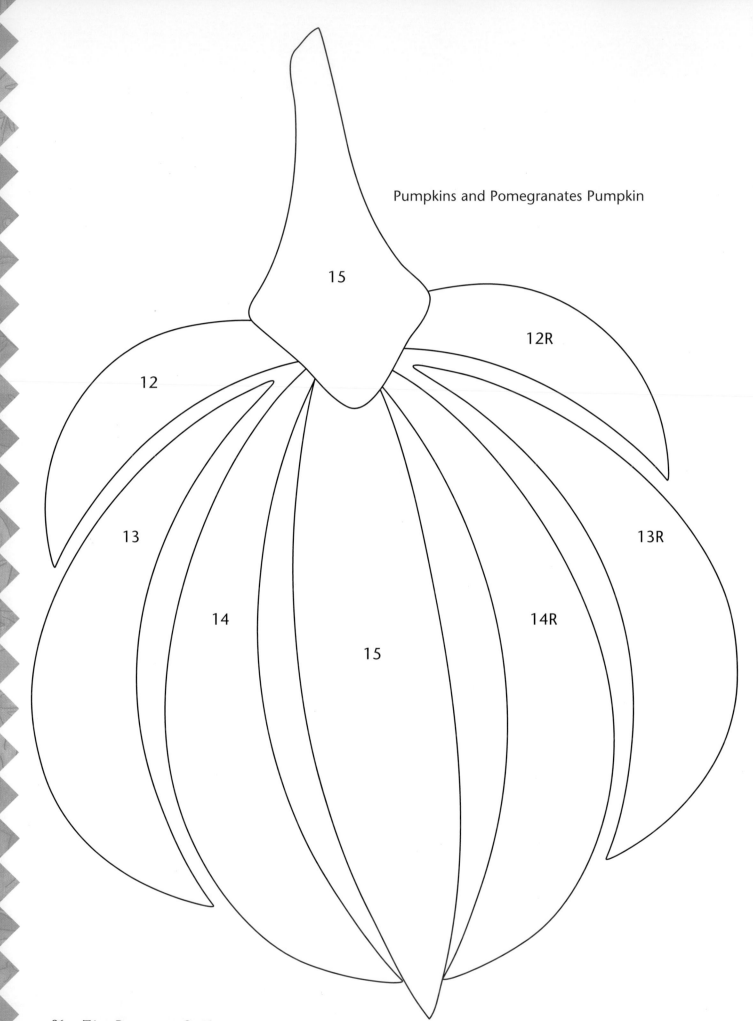

Pumpkins and Pomegranates Pumpkin

15

12R

12

13

13R

14

14R

15

Machine pieced and hand quilted by Jennifer Chiaverini, 2002.
*The fabrics were graciously donated by Benartex Fabrics.*

Finished Size: 50½" x 67½"
Block Size: 4" finished
Number of Blocks: 108 Four-Patch blocks

# UNDERGROUND
# RAILROAD QUILT

## FABRIC REQUIREMENTS

**Assorted lights to total:** $7/8$ yard

**Assorted darks to total:** $1\,1/4$ yards

**Assorted mediums to total:** $2/3$ yard

**Light background:** 1 yard

**Dark background:** $1\,1/2$ yards

**Backing:** $3\,1/8$ yards

**Batting:** 55" x 72"

**Binding:** $1/2$ yard

## Cutting

*Assorted lights:* Cut 120–$2\,1/2$" squares.

*Assorted mediums:* Cut 96–$2\,1/2$" squares.

*Assorted darks:* Cut 216–$2\,1/2$" squares.

*Light background:* Cut six $4\,7/8$"-wide strips. Cut the strips into forty-four squares, then cut each square in half diagonally to make eighty-eight half-square triangles.

*Dark background:* Cut six $4\,7/8$"-wide strips. Cut each strip into forty-four $4\,7/8$" squares, then cut each square in half diagonally to make 88 half-square triangles.

Cut two 7"-wide strips. Cut strips into ten 7" squares, then cut each square twice diagonally to make 40 setting triangles.

Cut one $3\,3/4$"-wide strip. Cut the strip into two $3\,3/4$" squares, then cut each square in half diagonally for the 4 corner triangles.

## Block Assembly

### Dark/Light Four-Patch Blocks

1. Sew a dark square to a light square. Press the seam toward the dark square.

2. Sew 2 units together to make 1 block. Press. Make 60.

*Dark/Light Four-Patch Make 60.*

### Dark/Medium Four-Patch Blocks

1. Sew a dark square to a medium square. Press the seam toward the dark square.

2. Sew 2 units together as shown to make 1 block. Press. Make 48.

*Dark/Medium Four-Patch Make 48.*

### Half-Square Triangle Blocks

Sew dark background triangles to light background triangles. Press the seams toward the dark triangles. Make 88.

*Half-square Triangles Make 88.*

## QUILT ASSEMBLY

1. Sew the side setting triangles, the Four-Patch blocks, and the half-square triangle blocks together into diagonal rows. Press the seams for each row in alternate directions. *Note: Alternate the Dark/Light and Medium/Dark Four-Patch blocks.*

2. Sew the diagonal rows together. Press.

3. Sew the 4 corner triangles to finish the top. Press.

4. Refer to Quilting 101, page 94, to layer the quilt top, batting, and backing; baste. Quilt as desired. Bind.

**Quilt Assembly Diagram**

Machine pieced and quilted by Nancy Odom, 2002.

*T*hen he held out the quilt to me and said, "I just wanted to tell you not to use this quilt no more." When I told him I did not understand, he looked away, paused, and added, "Too many people know about it. Someone talked...Do you get my meaning?"

Excerpted from *The Runaway Quilt*
by Jennifer Chiaverini

# QUILTING 101

**Seam Allowances:** A ¹⁄₄" seam allowance is used throughout. It's a good idea to do a test seam before you begin sewing to check that your ¹⁄₄" is accurate.

**Pressing:** In general, press seams toward the darker fabric. Press lightly in an up-and-down motion. Avoid using a very hot iron or over-ironing, which can distort shapes and blocks.

**Flying Geese:** With right sides together, sew a square to one side of the rectangle, using a diagonal seam. Trim the excess to a ¹⁄₄" seam allowance. Fold the square back and press along the diagonal seam. Sew a square to the opposite side of the rectangle, using a diagonal seam. Fold back and press along the diagonal seam; trim the excess fabric to a ¹⁄₄" seam allowance.

*Match the centers of both units.*

*Pin and sew the seam.*

**Curved Seams:** Mark the center of both units to be sewn together. Pin the pieces, right sides together, at the center point. Place a pin at each end of the sewing line. Pin the rest of the seam between the center pin and the pin at each end. Sew the pieces together. Press.

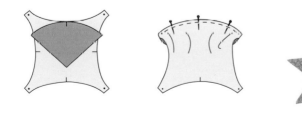

**Y-Seam Construction:** Mark a dot on the wrong side of the fabric ¹⁄₄" from the point of the triangle, and from the corner of each diamond. This is the starting and stopping point of the Y seam. Sew a diamond to the triangle unit. Backstitch at the dot. Press toward the diamond. Sew the other diamond to the opposite side of the triangle. Sew the two diamonds together, backstitching at the dot. Press.

*Mark dots on the triangle and diamonds.*

*Stitch to the dot and backstitch.*

*Press toward the diamond.*

Start ↓

← Backstitch at the dot

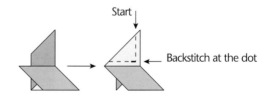

*Sew the other diamond to the triangle.*

Start ↓

← Backstitch at the dot

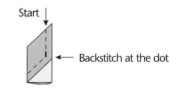

*Sew the 2 diamonds together.*

*Press.*

**Paper Piecing:** Once you get used to it, paper piecing is an easy way to ensure that your blocks will be accurate. You sew on the side of the paper with the printed lines. Fabric is placed on the non-printed side. With paper piecing you don't have to worry about the fabric grain. You are stitching on paper, which stabilizes the block. The paper is not removed until after the quilt top is together.

1. Trace or photocopy the number of paper-piecing patterns needed for your project.

2. Use a smaller-than-usual stitch length (1.5–1.8 or 18 to 20 stitches per inch), and a slightly larger needle (size 90/14). This makes the paper removal easier, and will result in tighter stitches that can't be pulled apart when you tear the paper off.

3. Cut the pieces slightly larger than necessary-about ³/₄" larger or more for triangles; they do not need to be perfect shapes. (One of the joys of paper piecing!)

4. Follow the number sequence when piecing. Pin piece #1 in place on the blank side of the paper, but make sure you don't place the pin anywhere near a seam line. Hold the paper up to the light to make sure the piece covers the area it is supposed to, with the seam allowance also amply covered.

5. Fold the pattern back at the stitching line and trim the fabric to a ¹/₄" seam allowance with a small acrylic ruler and rotary cutter.

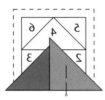

6. Cut piece #2 large enough to cover the area of #2 plus a generous seam allowance. It helps to cut each piece larger than you think necessary; it might be a bit wasteful, but easier than ripping out tiny stitches! Align the edge with the trimmed seam allowance of piece #1, right sides together, and pin. Paper side up, stitch one line.

7. Open piece #2 and press.

8. Continue stitching each piece in order, being sure to fold back the paper pattern and trim the seam allowance to ¹/₄" before adding the next piece.

9. Trim all around the finished unit to the ¹/₄" seam allowance. Leave the paper intact until after the blocks have been sewn together, then carefully remove it. Creasing the paper at the seam line helps when tearing it.

## Paper-Piecing Hints

- *When making several identical blocks, it helps to work in assembly line fashion. Add pieces #1 and #2 to each of the blocks, then add #3, and so on.*

- *Pre-cutting all the pieces at once is a time saver. Make one block first to ensure that each fabric piece will cover the area needed.*

- *Sometimes the seam allowance needs to be pressed toward the light fabric when dark and a light pieces are sewn together, and the edge of the dark seam allowance will sometimes show through the light fabric. To prevent this, trim the dark seam allowance about ¹/₁₆" narrower than the light seam allowance.*

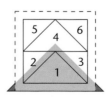

*Preparation for Appliqué:* To prepare the background for appliqué, lightly press the background block in half diagonally, vertically, and horizontally to find the center of the block and to create placement guidelines.

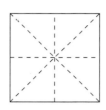

Using the patterns provided, trace each appliqué shape onto the template plastic and cut out on the line. Place the appliqué templates onto the background and lightly mark 1/8" the background inside the sewing line.

*Machine Appliqué Using Fusible-Web Adhesive:*
Lay the fusible web sheet paper-side up on the pattern and trace with a pencil. Trace detail lines with a permanent marker for ease in transferring to the fabric.

Use paper-cutting scissors to roughly cut out the pieces. Leave at least a 1/4" border.

Following the manufacturer's instructions, fuse the web patterns to the wrong side of the appliqué fabric. It helps to use an appliqué pressing sheet to avoid getting the adhesive on your iron or ironing board.

Cut out the pieces along the pencil line. Do not remove the paper yet.

Transfer the detail lines to the fabric by placing the piece on a light table or up to a window and marking the fabric. Use pencil for this task; the lines will be covered by thread.

Remove the paper and position the appliqué piece on your project. Be sure the web (rough) side is down. Fuse in place, following the manufacturer's instructions.

*Bias Strips:* Start with a square or rectangle of fabric. Place the ruler with the 45° mark on the left edge of the fabric. Make the first cut. Save the corner for your scrap

basket. Keeping the ruler parallel to the diagonal edge, measure the width of the strip needed and cut the first strip. Continue cutting diagonal strips for the length needed. The strip will be cut twice as wide as the finished strip, and 1/2" longer than the finished strip. Piece together with a diagonal seam as shown under Borders below.

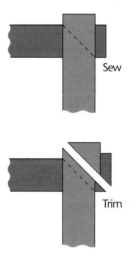

With wrong sides together, fold the bias strips in half lengthwise, and sew about 1/8" from the outside edge. Insert a bias bar, and press on both sides with the seam centered on the back. Remove the bias bar. Appliqué the bias strip in place with the seam down.

*Borders:* When borders strips are to be cut on the cross-wise grain, diagonally piece the strips together to achieve the needed lengths.

Sew

Trim

In most cases the side borders are sewn on first. When you have finished the quilt top, measure it through the center vertically. This will be the length to cut the side borders. Place pins at the centers of all four sides of the quilt top, as well as in the center of each side border strip. Pin the side borders to the quilt top first, matching the center pins. Using a 1/4" seam allowance, sew the borders to the quilt top and press.

Measure horizontally across the center of the quilt top including the side borders. This will be the length to cut the top and bottom borders. Repeat, pinning, sewing, and pressing.

*Backing:* Plan to make the backing a minimum of 2" larger than the quilt top on all sides. Prewash the fabric, and trim the selvages before you sew the backing sections together.

To economize, you can sew the back from any leftover fabrics or blocks in your collection.

*Batting:* The type of batting to use is a personal decision; consult your local quilt shop. Cut batting approximately 2" larger on all sides than your quilt top.

*Layering:* Spread the backing wrong side up and tape the edges down with masking tape. (If you are working on carpet you can use T-pins to secure the backing to the carpet.) Center the batting on top, smoothing out any folds. Place the quilt top right side up on top of the batting and backing, making sure it's centered.

*Basting:* If you plan to machine quilt, pin baste the quilt layers together with safety pins placed a minimum of 3"–4" apart. Begin basting in the center, and move toward the edges first in vertical, then horizontal, rows.

If you plan to hand quilt, baste the layers together with thread using a long needle and light-colored thread. Knot one end of the thread. Using stitches approximately the length of the needle, begin in the center and move out toward the edges.

*Quilting:* Quilting, whether by hand or machine, enhances the pieced or appliqué design of the quilt. You may choose to quilt in-the-ditch, echo the pieced or appliquéd motifs, use patterns from quilting design books and stencils, or do your own free-motion quilting.

*Double-Fold Straight Grain Binding (French Fold):*
Trim excess batting and backing from the quilt. If you want a 1/4" finished binding, cut the strips 2 1/4" wide and piece together with a diagonal seam to make a continuous binding strip.

Press the seams open, then press the entire strip in half lengthwise with wrong sides together. Fold the beginning end in 1/4". With raw edges even, pin the binding to the edge of the quilt a few inches away from the corner, and leave the first few inches of the binding unattached. Start sewing, using a 1/4" seam allowance.

Stop 1/4" away from the first corner, and backstitch one stitch. Lift the presser foot and rotate the quilt. Fold the binding at a right angle so it extends straight above the quilt. Then bring the binding strip down even with the edge of the quilt. Begin sewing at the folded edge. When you reach the beginning, tuck the end into the fold of the unfinished part of the binding. Pin one layer to the front of the quilt top, stitch to the front. Fold the binding to the back, and whipstitch around the perimeter of the quilt.

1/4"

*Stitch to 1/4" from corner.*

*First fold for miter*

*Second fold alignment.
Repeat in the same manner at all corners.*

# INDEX/RESOURCES

## RESOURCES

Anderson, Alex. *Start Quilting with Alex Anderson, 2nd ed.: Six Projects for First-Time Quilters,* Lafayette, CA: C&T Publishing, 2001.

Anderson, Alex. *Hand Quilting with Alex Anderson,* Lafayette, CA: C&T Publishing, 1998.

Hargrave, Harriet & Sharyn Craig. *The Art of Classic Quiltmaking,* Lafayette, CA: C&T Publishing, 2000.

Hargrave, Harriet. *Mastering Machine Appliqué, 2nd ed.,* Lafayette, CA: C&T Publishing, 2002.

# About the AUTHORS

Jennifer Chiaverini lives with her husband and son in Madison, Wisconsin, where she quilts with the Mad City Quilters.

Quilt designer, author, and teacher Nancy Odom has 27 patterns and 6 books in publication, with more pattern and book ideas always in the works. Also among her creations are Quilter's Gloves™ for the machine quilter. Her company, Timid Thimble Creations, markets her products.

Nancy has appeared on three episodes of *Simply Quilts* with Alex Anderson and on *America Sews* with Sue Hausmann. Nancy's *When You Believe*, a Christmas series quilt for *McCall's Quilting* magazine, was featured in the last three issues of 2000. She has also created quilts for C&T Publishing, Hoffman Fabrics, Benartex Fabrics, and Viking Sewing Machines. Nancy is a featured teacher and lecturer at quilt shows, quilt guilds, and quilt shops around the country.

Nancy completed her first quilt at the age of 17. She credits her grandmother's love of quilting for inspiring her at such a young age. She has vivid memories of sneaking downstairs after "bedtime" as a child to watch her grandmother appliqué a quilt top. Today, the very quilt that inspired that little girl has a proud place among Nancy's own quilted creations.

Natives of northwest Florida, Nancy and her husband Jim have five children and three grandchildren. Carmel, Indiana (just north of Indianapolis) is their current home.

## LOOK FOR JENNIFER CHIAVERINI'S ELM CREEK QUILTS NOVELS BY SIMON & SCHUSTER:

*The Quilter's Apprentice*

*Round Robin*

*The Cross-Country Quilters*

*The Runaway Quilt*

COMING IN MARCH 2003: *The Quilter's Legacy*

## OTHER FINE BOOKS FROM C&T PUBLISHING:

*Appliqué 12 Easy Ways! Charming Quilts, Giftable Projects & Timeless Techniques,* Elly Sienkiewicz

*The Art of Classic Quiltmaking,* Harriet Hargrave and Sharyn Craig

*The Art of Machine Piecing: Quality Workmanship Through a Colorful Journey,* Sally Collins

*Civil War Women: Their Quilts, Their Roles, and Activities for Re-Enactors,* Barbara Brackman

*Hand Appliqué with Alex Anderson: Seven Projects for Hand Appliqué,* Alex Anderson

*Hand Quilting with Alex Anderson: Six Projects for Hand Quilters,* Alex Anderson

*Heirloom Machine Quilting, Third Ed.,* Harriet Hargrave

*Mastering Machine Appliqué, 2nd ed.,* Harriet Hargrave

*Quilts, Quilts, and More Quilts!* Diana McClun and Laura Nownes

*Show Me How to Machine Quilt: A Fun, No-Mark Approach,* Kathy Sandbach

**For more information write for a free catalog:**

C&T Publishing, Inc.
P.O. Box 1456
Lafayette, CA 94549
(800) 284-1114
e-mail: ctinfo@ctpub.com
website: www.ctpub.com

**For quilting supplies:**

Cotton Patch Mail Order
3405 Hall Lane, Dept. CTB
Lafayette, CA 94549
(800) 835-4418
(925) 283-7883
e-mail: quiltusa@yahoo.com
website: www.quiltusa.com

*Note: Fabrics used in the quilts shown may not be currently available since fabric manufacturers keep most fabrics in print for only a short time.*